TED WILLIAMS
FIRST LATINO IN THE BASEBALL HALL OF FAME

BILL NOWLIN

Rounder Books

Ted Williams: First Latino in the Baseball Hall of Fame
By Bill Nowlin
Copyright 2018 by Bill Nowlin

ISBNs
978-1-57940-255-6 Ted Williams – *First Latino in the Baseball Hall of Fame*
978-1-57940-011-8 Ted Williams – *First Latino in the Baseball Hall of Fame*
(e-book edition)

Cover and book design by Rachael Sullivan

Biography
Baseball
Ted Williams
First edition

Rounder Books
29 Lancaster Street
Cambridge, Massachusetts 02140

TED WILLIAMS

FIRST **LATINO** IN THE BASEBALL HALL OF FAME

BY BILL NOWLIN

Ted, May and Danny Williams, about 1921.

The news that Ted Williams had Hispanic blood - that he was really the first Latino inducted into the National Baseball Hall of Fame - takes a lot of people by surprise. I've had a couple of articles published on the subject, and they elicited quite a surprised response. Of course, his family knew it all along. They just never made much fuss about it, and neither did he.

Ted's maternal grandparents emigrated to the United States from Mexico. A couple of sentences in Ted's autobiography *My Turn At Bat* caught my attention, but there didn't seem to be a lot to go on. Ted had written, "Her maiden name was Venzer, she was part Mexican and part French, and that's fate for you; if I had had my mother's name, there is no doubt I would have run into problems in those days, the prejudices people had in Southern California." Ted wrote that on page 28, and that was about all he ever had to say about his Hispanic heritage.

It may have been a heritage he never wanted known, because of those very prejudices.

I wanted to pursue this further, though, so back in 1997 when I was working on my first book about Ted Williams, I did a nationwide web search on the name Venzer. There were five people listed. I called them up. They didn't know anything about having Ted Williams as a relative. There was no thread for me to follow. So I gave up. I made reference to Ted's Hispanic heritage, saying "Ted's mother May Venzer Williams, originally from El Paso, gave Ted his Mexican blood." That was about it.

I asked some of his childhood friends about it when I visited with several of them in April of 1997. Joe Villarino had played ball with Ted in San Diego, as far back as the third grade at Garfield Elementary School. Joe's father, he told me, came from Mexico. Asked about Ted's mother May, Villarino said, "His mother was Mexican. I'm a Mexican -- my dad was Mexican and my mother Spanish. Once in a while somebody will ask me about Ted's mother, and if she was Mexican. They didn't believe it, because Ted, you know, he had no signs of being a Mexican at all."[1] I had never doubted it, since Ted had said so in *My Turn At Bat*, but it was good to confirm that Ted did have an Hispanic heritage. I kept hoping to learn more.

A THREAD TO FOLLOW

My first book on Ted was one I co-authored with Jim Prime. It was published by Masters Press and named *Ted Williams: A Tribute*. The book came out in November, 1997, a little late in the year to get good distribution - but out it came. (The book was later republished as *Ted Williams: The Pursuit of Perfection* by Sports Publishing, in 2002.) Nearly a year and a half later, Jim received an e-mail out of the blue from Manuel Herrera, informing Jim that he (Herrera, not Prime) was Ted Williams' cousin. We'd received a few notes we'd had to treat with skepticism, but Jim passed this right on to me, knowing of my interest in this aspect of the Ted Williams story. I wrote Mr. Herrera that I was responding to the note he'd sent Jim and asked him for more information about himself, and asked if I could call him and do an interview. He replied positively, and sent me his phone number.

On May 29, 1999 I phoned him and we talked for a full hour. Manuel filled me in on a lot of history on Ted's mother's side of the family - and even told me that Ted's mother's sister, his Aunt Sarah Diaz, was still living at age 94 in Santa Barbara. It was maybe seven or eight minutes into the interview before he used the name Venzor. Venzor? Venz-oar? As I transcribed the tape later, I kept hearing him say "Venzor" -- not "Venzer", which I'd always been pronouncing "Venz-air." Accent on the first syllable. Part Mexican and part French, Ted had written. Either way, that would be the way it was pronounced. But this was clearly "Venz-oar" – again, with the accent on the second syllable. I pulled out a copy of Ted's birth certificate, which was reproduced on page 2 of Dick Johnson and Glenn Stout's 1991 book *Ted Williams: A Portrait in Words and Pictures.* There it was, clear as anything: Venzor. Yet in the text right on the very next page, the authors use the name "Venzer." Why wouldn't they? After all, that's the way Ted spelled it in his own autobiography.

Who would think that Ted would misspell his own mother's maiden name? Of course, the truth is he might not have done anything of the sort. First of all, the autobiography was written by Ted Williams with John Underwood. John spent a LOT of time with Ted and ended up collaborating on three books with him – *My Turn At Bat, The Science of Hitting* and *Fishing the Big Three.* What a pleasure that must have been. Underwood is a talented professional writer who came to know Ted Williams well, and helped produce some excellent work. Both *My Turn At Bat* and *The Science of Hitting* are classics, and have been in print from one of the world's largest publishing houses for over 30 years. That doesn't happen with many books. But it would have been John Underwood who did all the actual writing, all the typing and probably the final proofreading. My guess is that he heard the way Ted pronounced his mother's name, and Ted probably pronounced it in his Southern California way, not with the intonation a Spanish-speaker would have used. When I had an opportunity to talk with Ted himself over dinner at his home, he did indeed pronounce the family name "Venz-urr" – with the accent on the first syllable. Underwood probably heard that and, quite reasonably, wrote Venzer. And Ted never spotted it, if and when he proofread the manuscript.

In late 2002, I wrote John and asked him if he thought this might have been what happened. He wrote back, "Regarding the family name, I'd say -- without really knowing, you understand -- that your take on it is correct."[2]

Interestingly, Ed Linn took *My Turn At Bat* as gospel and even wrote in his biography *Hitter* that the birth certificate had misspelled her name as Venzor.[3]

Manuel Herrera.

However it came to be, from 1969 when *My Turn At Bat* first was printed, anyone wanting to research Ted's family history would have read his mother's name as Venzer and accepted that as correct. If anyone noticed the discrepancy between the birth certificate and the autobiography, they would have been likely to figure that Ted's spelling was correct and that the clerk who completed the birth certificate had erred. After all, it was Ted's autobiography. And clerks do make errors.

After I finished interviewing Manuel Herrera, and as I transcribed the cassette tape from our phone conversation, I realized the depth of information he had revealed and I was astounded. None of this was in any of the many books about Ted Williams. Manuel was, and remains, an energetic fount of information. He'd never written this all down, but he had soaked up and retained a full family history in his head.

RESEARCHING THE FAMILY

At this point, I did two things. First of all, I telephoned Sarah Diaz. She was 94. I didn't waste any time. I phoned her within a day or two. She was articulate and had a wonderful memory, and we talked for a full hour as well. She was a Venzor herself. May Venzor's younger sister. In our talk, she came across as a wonderful woman of the West and I thoroughly enjoyed our conversation. Everything Manuel had told me jibed with what Aunt Sarah recounted. And there were many family members they'd both referred to. Off and on over the next three years, I contacted a number of family members and filled in my knowledge as best I could. When I did a web search on Venzor, there were a lot of them. There were 37 listings in California. I knew May Venzor had been born in El Paso; there were 114 listings in Texas. The main outlines of the Venzor family history came from Aunt Sarah and Ted's cousin Manuel Herrera, and in speaking with numerous other relatives since, the information they provided has only been augmented and elaborated, never contradicted.

Arnold Diaz, Ted and his aunt Sarah, Santa Barbara.

Then, nearly a year later, in 2000, I learned that one of Ted's uncles was still living, in El Paso. I'm a member of the Society for American Baseball Research (SABR) and SABR offers a very active online chat list for its members. At some point in April 2000, the subject of Ted Williams' Mexican ancestry came up. Eric Enders, a researcher at the Hall of Fame in Cooperstown, had written in about the subject, so I dropped Eric a note and we traded a few e-mails. Eric comes from El Paso himself, and recalled a local newspaper column about Ted's uncle living there. This was fascinating, because Ted Williams' birth certificate said that May Venzor Williams had been born in El Paso. An uncle in El Paso made perfect sense, and seemed to offer new vistas.

Eric was able to locate the article for me, written by Ray Sanchez of the *El Paso Herald-Post*, and it supplied the uncle's name: Ernesto Ponce. Well, there was no Ernesto Ponce listed, but I tried entering "Ernest" and struck paydirt.

I called him up and conducted another telephone interview. This gave me more information, but it was a more difficult conversation - not as fluid as I would have liked. I figured if I'd have the opportunity to meet him in person, I could probably learn a lot more.

Since I'd never been to El Paso (but always loved the Marty Robbins song), I decided to visit. My wife Yleana came from Laredo, another Texas border community, and I'd enjoyed many visits there

Ernesto Ponce, handball player.

11

Eulalia and Federico Ponce.

(and even taken in baseball games on both sides of the border – Laredo and Nuevo Laredo.) It could be interesting to visit El Paso. Besides, how many people in the last year of the twentieth century were ever going to get the chance to visit Ted Williams' uncle? Ted himself was still living; he was 82 at the time.

The year before, 1999, I had hoped to visit Sarah Diaz in Santa Barbara, booked my flights for later in June and made my arrangements. Manuel Herrera suggested a number of people in town I should seek out. At the last minute, though, Sarah got cold feet and requested that I not come. Ted had always been very private about his family, and while she had been very forthcoming over the telephone, perhaps the prospect of my coming to visit left her feeling a bit of trepidation. I could understand that. After all, Ted might not like her to be divulging all this information, and the family had never been ones to publicize their famous relation. I tried to reassure her, and also spoke with Dee Allen, her niece who lived nearby, but in vain. I was disappointed, but naturally respected her decision.

Sarah Diaz died on November 3, 1999. I never met Aunt Sarah, which I truly regret, but I did make my way to El Paso, in Texas, on Election Day 2000 -- the election it seemed would never end. Weeks later, they were still counting and recounting ballots in Florida. I'd voted absentee.

The day after the election, I visited the Ponces -- Ernie and his wife Mary, and we had a good chance to talk. I'd also been in touch with another relative in the area, Kathleen Osowski. She is Manuel Herrera's sister and though she only lived a few miles away from the Ponces had never met them. I visited her at her real estate office, and Kathleen and I drove up the mountain together for the visit and had a chance to meet Ted's uncle and aunt that morning. Ernie was wearing a New York Mets cap, and I gave him a bit of a hard time about that, but both Mary and Ernie told me of their honeymoon to San Diego in the 1930s and told me more about the family and their own stories. Later in the day, after I spent a couple of hours in Juarez across the border, I enjoyed dinner with Kathleen and her husband.

Ernest Ponce, it turns out, served on the El Paso City Council from 1951 to 1957, the first Hispanic council member in the city's history. There was once a time that he played against John Wayne in a handball tournament in Hollywood. John Wayne asked him, "You really play to win, don't you?" "Yes, sir. I'm going to hit the ball where you're not," was the reply.[4]

Eric Enders and I coincidentally both met in Toronto a few months later, on our way to Cuba where we spent a week on a Cubaball tour, taking in five Cuban baseball games and doing some research there. Two different hotels - the Sevilla and the Nacional -- had photographs of Ted Williams in their lobbies. I was also able to find three different photos of Ted in Cuba from street vendors or private collectors. Pre-Castro, Ted had thought about retiring to the Varadero area on Cuba's north coast. But that's another story.[5]

Throughout all of this, I kept in touch with Manuel. We have traded a few hundred e-mails. He is an amazing repository of family knowledge. He has an encyclopedic mind and a good memory for story after story after story. Family clearly means a lot to him and he seems to have absorbed and remembered a wealth of information. He can spin out stories and genealogies like the honored *griots* of western Africa, who rely on their prodigious memories to pass the stories of their clans and the lore of their villages down from generation to generation. Every family should have a keeper of tradition like Manuel Herrera.

So what is the story? Enough of the introduction.

TED'S RETICENCE ABOUT HIS FAMILY

Ted Williams wrote little about his family. And he didn't like prying newspapermen. When he first arrived in Boston, he was the talk of the town. He was a fresh, enthusiastic kid full of vim and vigor and an overflowing love of playing the game of baseball. This was the youngster who would wake up his veteran San Diego Padres roommate Cedric Durst at 6:00 in the morning, practicing his batting swing in the hotel room, with a rolled-up newspaper, crowing, "Christ, Ced, it's great to be young and full of vinegar!"

This was "The Kid," who would be in a reverie in right field (he played right field in 1939, his first year with Boston) swinging at imagined pitches, while he was supposed to be setting himself defensively for the opposing batter. This was the lanky colt most baseball fans have seen in the old film clip (and most have seen it a dozen or more times) who, in his third year in the majors, was still so unaffected he truly leapt around the bases, galloping and bouncing and clapping his hands after hitting the home run to win the 1941 All-Star Game for his fellow American Leaguers.

But The Kid had grown wary. After his honeymoon season in 1939, when he set a rookie record for runs batted in (145) which has never been topped, reporters wanted more stories about Teddy Williams. Ted had already made one enemy in the press, by declining an interview with one of the deans – Bill Cunningham – because Cunningham was intoxicated. Ted's mother May was a soldier in the Salvation Army, staunchly opposed to drink, and Ted himself shunned alcohol for many years. He didn't have much patience for drunks. When Cunningham approached Ted in a Florida hotel lobby, he was obviously inebriated. Red Sox pitcher Elden Auker told me, "Ted looked up at him and said, 'I'm sorry, Mr. Cunningham, I don't give interviews to sportswriters that are drinking.' And boy, you could have...this just embarrassed Cunningham terribly. In front of all of us....Cunningham spent the rest of his sportswriting days trying to hurt Ted and I think the rest of them kind of copied what he'd done." [6]

Ted struggles with a Mexican outfit during a Texas Rangers game.

Boston was a highly competitive newspaper town, with many editors vying for stories to sell papers and many reporters eager to please. One or two enterprising reporters made their way to Ted's home in San Diego and started asking questions. Where was Ted? He wasn't in San Diego. They learned he was in Minnesota, visiting a girl he'd met there and enjoying some hunting and some fishing. This was Doris Soule, whom Ted later married. Her father was a hunting guide. With no Ted, they started asking questions of his mother: why didn't Ted come home to see you? How much money did he send home?

These days, with all the supermarket tabloids and with any number of television programs tapping the same vein, these questions would almost be expected. Par for the course. In those days, they were really beyond the pale. Many of the writers partook of the same temptations offered the ballplayers, and the personal lives of players were pretty much off-limits. Ted

Young Danny Williams, on the Salvation Army drum.

resented this prying, this intrusion into his family life. Ed Linn suggests that a Harold Kaese column in the *Boston Transcript* in May 1940, was perhaps the last straw. Ted wasn't hitting well. That always upset him. Kaese quoted manager Joe Cronin and a couple of Ted's teammates as critical of The Kid's lackadaisical fielding, and accused Ted of "extreme selfishness, egoism and lack of courage," adding (Kaese supposedly tried to retract this latter part prior to publication), "Whatever it is, it probably traces to his upbringing. Can you imagine a kid, a nice kid with a nimble brain not visiting his father and mother all of last winter."[7]

This sort of thing turned Ted against newspaper writers for the rest of his life. He had some vicious things to say about some of the writers, and it was only well after he'd finished his career that he reached some guarded accommodation with the "knights of the keyboard." Needless to say, many of the writers struck back and took out their resentments one way or another – denying Williams a vote for MVP, creating columns condemning his approach to the game, and the like.

Another player might shrug off stories nosing into his relationship with his family. The ferocity of Ted's reaction to these stories, though, betrayed his conflicted feelings about family. Bluntly, Ted was embarrassed and even ashamed of his family, so it infuriated him when writers started turning over rocks to see what they might uncover. He became enraged, because he was ashamed, and he couldn't just let it go.

One of the reasons *My Turn At Bat* is such a remarkable book is that John Underwood was able to get Ted to be so honest about his feelings. It was one of the first sports biographies where a player was willing to open up and admit to personal vulnerabilities. To Underwood, Ted talked about his family as candidly as a writer could hope. He wrote that his father had served in the Army and perhaps in combat. "Whenever anybody wrote about my dad they seemed to delight in calling him a 'wanderer' or a 'deserter of the family,' but that's a lot of bull. He stuck it out with my mother for twenty years, and finally he packed up, and I'd probably have done the same." Some say that Ted in effect did do the same; he rarely made visits home, even in his mother's declining years. "My mother was a wonderful woman in many ways," he continued, "but, gee, I wouldn't have wanted to be married to a woman like that. Always gone. The house dirty all the time....She was religious to the point of being domineering, and so narrow-minded....My mother had a lot of traits that made me cringe." Still, despite all that, "My dad and I were never close. I was always closer to my mother, always feeling I had to do right by her, always feeling she was alone, and knowing for years afterward how hard she had worked with nothing to show for it. I loved my dad, it wasn't that I didn't love him. But he didn't push very hard. He was just satisfied to let things go as they were."[8]

Ted Williams was forthright and honest. He admitted his own shortcomings, and laid bare a lot of the disappointment he felt about his own childhood and his own family. He told of being closer to other fathers in the neighborhood than to his own father. He told how humiliated he felt when his mother continually dragged him to Salvation Army events, making him march with the band. He let us know about his younger brother Danny, who always seemed to be getting into trouble.

Some of his classmates ribbed him about his mother and he had flushed with shame. He didn't have a happy home. His family was deteriorating around him by the mid to late 1930s. His parents' marriage had effectively dissolved and his brother was becoming more difficult, hanging out with "an altogether different bunch," and always in "some kind of scrape." He knew that Rod Luscomb had taken a loaded revolver off of Danny one time. Ted, though, had his girlfriend in Princeton, Minnesota. He had fashioned a new life for himself in professional baseball; the players were his peers. He really didn't have sufficient reason to want to go home. And so, being Ted Williams and becoming more and more accustomed to doing things his own way, he did not.

Years later, in 1992, Ted visited the Utah Street house with his son John-Henry Williams. The current owner, Terry Higgins, gladly admitted them, but could sense Ted's reluctance. Higgins said, "This house, Ted don't like it. You could see it brought back a lot of bad memories. All he wanted to do was get out...This house, Ted don't like it at all."[9]

TED'S FATHER, SAMUEL STUART WILLIAMS –
A NEW YORK YANKEE

Before getting to the story of Ted Williams' Latino heritage, let's look at his father. Like Ted, his father struck out on his own, too, at an early age. Not a lot is known about Ted's father. He's a very difficult guy to research. Ted had relatively little to say about his dad in *My Turn At Bat*, and the impression he conveyed didn't come across all that well, though on a closer reading some of what Ted had to say was not unkind. "I loved my dad," he wrote. "It wasn't that I didn't love him. But he didn't push very hard. He was just satisfied to let things go as they were." No one ever said that about Ted Williams.

Samuel S. Williams.

When was Samuel Stuart Williams born, and what was his family like? A researcher wanting to learn more probably starts with the famous Ted Williams birth certificate.

It offers his father's name as Samuel S. Williams, a place of birth (Ardsley NY) and the fact that Samuel Williams was 32 years of age at his last birthday. Ted was born at the Sunshine Maternity Home on August 30, 1918. Or maybe August 20. His birthday was always celebrated on the 30th, but the more likely date may be the 20th. The typed data on Ted's birth certificate provides the date as August 20, 1918. At some later time, the "20" was crossed out and replaced with a hand-written "30." Dr. J. M. Steade was the physician; whoever prepared the form dated it August 21, making the 20th a more likely date. It was filed September 4, 1918 with the Bureau of Vital Statistics of the California State Board of Health.

The *San Diego Evening Tribune* in 1937 listed his birth date as October 30, but it seems that Ted just made that date up. Biographer Michael Seidel's explanation: "he just didn't relish the distraction during the season."[10] Harold Kaese of the *Boston Globe* says that Ted told him, way back in his rookie year 1939, that he was born at the end of August, but moved his birth date back two months, "because I didn't want to celebrate my birthday during the playing season." Ted was, if nothing else, determined to learn everything he could about baseball, and to avoid anything that might prove distracting -- such as people making a fuss about his birthday during the season. As Kaese concluded, "He thought of everything, even when he was a kid."[11] Whether Ted's birthday was the 20th or 30th may remain uncertain; the date of filing of the birth certificate and The Kid's admission to Kaese should both effectively rule out the October date. For what it's worth, Ted's official high school record bears the date of 8/30/18. So do his military records, both those he completed during World War II and those when he was recalled to service for the Korean War.

What about Ted's father, and *his* birth, though? None of the books on Ted Williams offered much of any information. Teddy's birth certificate provided the only clue - that he was said to be 32 when Teddy was born. If Samuel Williams was born, say, in April, and was 32 years or age in 1918, then he himself would have been born in 1886. If he'd been born sometime after August 20 or 30, then perhaps he'd been born in 1885.

Maybe a search of birth records in Ardsley, New York would provide the answers. The first problem encountered, though, loomed large: there was no Ardsley, New York, in the 1880s. George Calvi, Ardsley Village Manager, wrote me, "Ardsley was not an incorporated village prior to 1896." Well, OK, the Ted Williams birth certificate was from 1918, and Ardsley existed by that time. Sam Williams might still have had family there, and even though he himself was born in – perhaps – Dobbs Ferry or Yonkers or another community, the rest of his family might in 1918 have lived in the newly-named Ardsley, and he may therefore have chosen the current name rather than the name the community had been known by in the days when he'd been born.

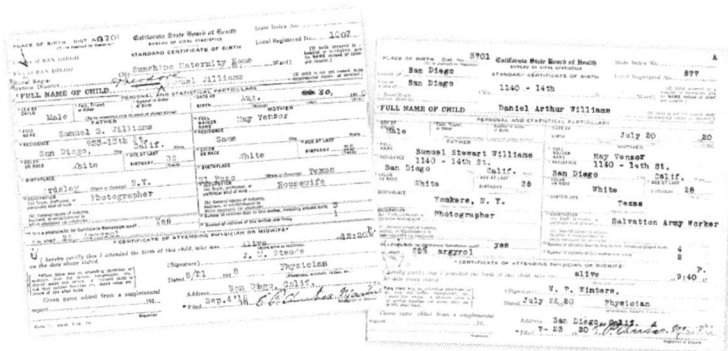

Birth certificates: Ted Williams and Danny Williams.

Again, tapping the network of researchers which SABR offers, I came in contact with Frank Jazzo, who lives in the area. I told Frank what I had to go on, and he researched local town records for a Samuel Williams, born around this time period. Frank is the Town Historian of Tarrytown, New York, and Frank found a record of a Samuel Williams' birth, writing me of the find on the man's actual birthday. "Happy Birthday, Sam Williams," Frank wrote me on June 8, 2002. "Happy Birthday, Samuel Williams, born June 8, 1886, in Tarrytown, N.Y., 5th child of John Williams & Josephine DeRevre Williams." Frank's research showed that Samuel was actually born in Glenville, a section of the Town of Greenburgh, with a Tarrytown post office address (things are complicated in this part of New York state.)

Wow! I was sure he'd found it. It all fit, even to the point of a sister named Florence, who I figured might have been Ted's Aunt Effie. More on her later. Where could I take this information? With this additional bit of data, there were more avenues I could explore. Williams is such a common name that it presents the problem of an overwhelming number of possibilities. DeRevre, though – that's an unusual name. I did a web search and found a book on management by Marc Van DeRevre. I thought it sounded like kind of a Belgian name, and a business associate of mine in The Netherlands agreed. But Mr. Van DeRevre never wrote back. Not that much to go on, really. I was so sure that we had found the right guy, though, that I sent off a note to Ted's son John-Henry Williams, letting him know of his grandfather's birthday. I didn't get a reply from him, either.

Ted Williams died less than a month after Frank Jazzo's note. There was no funeral service held, but a celebration of Ted's life was held on July 22, 2002 at Fenway Park in Boston. Ted's two nephews – his brother Danny's two sons, Sam Williams and Ted Williams, both attended and I had the opportunity to visit with them at their hotel on July 21 and then on the field and in the park the day of the event itself.

I had been looking for them for years – asking everyone I could if they knew how to locate them. Ted Williams Family Enterprises was of no assistance;

I'm not sure how hard they tried. I even went so far as to do an internet search for everyone in the entire country named Theodore Williams and Samuel Williams and actually phoned every single one of the California listings, back in 2000, but turned up nothing. I seemed to have hit a dead end. I'd heard that one of them played guitar and that one had gone to Cal Poly at San Luis Obispo. There was a classical guitarist named Ted Williams, but he let me know he wasn't the right man. The Cal Poly alumni office was unable to help. Then suddenly, an article by Joseph Kahn in the *Boston Globe*

mentioned that both nephews were coming to the Fenway event. Apparently they had contacted the Red Sox, who put them in touch with club historian Dick Bresciani. Bresh let the *Globe* know, and Joe mentioned them in print. I contacted Joe and he told me how to reach nephew Ted, so I called and in turn spoke to both Ted and Sam, and we met up at their hotel in Boston once they arrived.

May Williams with her grandchildren, Ted and Sam Williams, at Sarah's house in Santa Barbara, 1958.

When we met, I gave them each one a copy of *Ted Williams: The Pursuit of Perfection,* which had been republished in a new edition eight days before Ted died. The book was a revised and expanded version of our earlier *Ted Williams: A Tribute.* I met Sam and Ted again (and Ted's son Noah) the next morning at the Fenway Park event and we walked around the field. I was able to introduce them in person to Dick Bresciani and also to Leigh Montville, who had begun work on a biography of Ted for Doubleday about six months before Ted died. For sons of the brother (Daniel Arthur Williams), the brother who bore the burden of a bad reputation in all the books on Ted Williams, they both seemed very nice guys. And they were both frank in their memories of their father, readily admitting there was much about him they did not know. Had Danny Williams spent time behind bars? Had he been discharged from the Army for going AWOL to see his wife? They weren't sure, but they'd heard stories. They didn't dismiss the possibilities, nor were they defensive. Both were aware that aunts and family in Texas knew more about Danny Williams, but the family diverted even their questions on the subject.

Their own memories of their father were of a hard-working man, who seemed to move house often for reasons unknown – they wondered, was he dodging creditors? – until he got sick with cancer, wasted away and died when both were relatively young. Ted paid for his brother's cancer treatment, including air flights for treatment with specialists. Danny was, as I understand it, conflicted. He needed the financial assistance but, we can appreciate, resented his dependency. When Danny died during Ted's last season as a major league ballplayer, 1960, his two sons were both less than 10 years old. Ironically, uncle Ted had for years been the leading celebrity raising funds to fight cancer in children for Boston's Jimmy Fund. It was at Children's Hospital in Boston that the first breakthroughs in the treatment of leukemia were achieved. Ted had been actively helping raise money to fight leukemia since the late 1940s. Unfortunately, Ted's own son John-Henry Williams would let it be known in October 2003, at age 35, that he himself had been stricken with acute myelogenous leukemia. Despite a bone marrow transplant from his sister Claudia, John-Henry died of the disease on March 6, 2004.

The relationship between Ted and Danny was not uniformly unfriendly, though, as one might have assumed from what has been written. Danny's son Ted remembers many phone calls between the two, and that they were much closer and more loving toward each other than an outside reader ever would have guessed.

Ted promised Danny and his wife Jean that he would ensure their boys could have something he never had: a college education. Sam became a musician and traveled up and down the West Coast as a guitarist and folksinger; he never took Uncle Ted up on the offer. But John Theodore "Ted" Williams did. He's the one who went to college, and become a graphic designer with his own firm in the Bay Area. Sam Williams became...of all things, a sportswriter! Sam works for the *Lassen County Times* in Susanville, California, and as of 2014 was the managing editor of the newspaper.

Given the negative image that Ted's son John-Henry built up over the years, it may seem ironic that the sons of the "bad seed" grew up humble, unassuming, and decent men. Talking with them and learning about family from their perspective was a pleasure. They seemed as curious as I was to learn more about their famous uncle and his family background.

SOME DOCUMENTATION ON SAMUEL WILLIAMS

After he returned back home to Oakland, California, Ted (the nephew) mailed me copies of grandfather Samuel Williams' military papers. Those provided their own bits of information.

Among other documents Ted had was a copy of his father Danny's birth certificate. On Danny's birth certificate, Samuel Williams' birthplace is listed as Yonkers, NY. In 1918, he told them it was Ardsley but in 1920 he said it was Yonkers. Was he trying to confuse later historians? Sam now stated his age as 35; given Danny's birth date of July 20, 1920, this suggests that Sam was born in 1885.

I was later able to obtain copies of Samuel S. Williams' Social Security application and his death certificate. The former one, he completed. The latter was, inevitably, completed for him. His Social Security application was made on March 1, 1940. He was still married to May at the time, but he had already left the family home and was living in the Navarra Hotel at 402 Stockton Street in San Francisco. On the form, he gives his parents' names as Nicholas Williams and Elizabeth Miller. He declared his birth date as April 5, 1895. Not 1885. Had he missed the right year by a decade? Though a photographer by trade, who had run his own studio in downtown San Diego, he had no employer at the time of application. He still had a little trouble with ages. Under "age at last birthday" he seems to have written 45, then changed it to 46, then crossed it all out and entered "44."

After his divorce from May, Sam married Minnie Mae Dickson, who had worked with him as his assistant.

From his obituary, I learned the name of the funeral home which had arranged Samuel Williams' burial; it still operates under a somewhat different name today as Hull's Walnut Creek Chapel, but Mark Hull – son of the man who ran it in 1952 – graciously faxed me a copy of the funeral record. It's a family firm dating back to 1892, I learned during a personal visit to the funeral home in November 2002. I thought it was an odd touch that a rack outside the director's office featured color postcards of the facility. Be that as it may, office manager Bob Carroll didn't hesitate to additionally supply me with a copy of Minnie Williams' funeral record. Ted Williams and I both visited the graves of his paternal grandparents Samuel and Minnie Williams at Colma, California.

Information for Samuel's record was supplied by the informant, his widow, Minnie. There it states that he was born April 5, 1883 – though the "3" has been written in over a typed number which looks like an "8." Age (last birthday) reads, clearly, "69" but the final digit is altered as well from another number - obviously a lesser one. If he was 69 when he died on November 16, 1952, and only 44 when he applied for his Social Security card in 1940, somehow he gained 25 years between two years which most people would consider 12 years apart. The death certificate, interestingly, also states "yes" in response to the question, "Was deceased ever in U. S. armed forces?" but then adds the comment, "No war." Assuming that this was not an early manifestation of the anti-war sentiment characteristic of the Bay Area in the late 1960s, it seems to reflect that his widow did not know about his military service, or was intending to inform us that her husband had not served in a declared war.

A visit to the Westchester County archives and the Clerk's Office of the Town of Greenburgh, New York, revealed that many nineteenth century births were not noted at all in contemporary records. Apparently birth registration was voluntary and many families simply didn't bother.

Might there have been other relatives of Samuel Williams, whose descendants would have a family Bible or other genealogy? There might be. But I haven't found them yet. Complicating research into Sam Williams' upbringing is that he was said to have run away from home, or at least – as Ted Williams wrote – "run off and joined the Army."[12]

The varying dates given for Sam Williams' birth might reflect a desire to portray himself as older at one stage in his life – perhaps to obtain employment or to enlist in the Army -- and younger at another point, for whatever reason. According to his military discharge papers, Sam Williams was a shipbuilder at the time of his enlistment and was 21 7/12 years old on December 6, 1904, the date of his enlistment at Yonkers, NY. He was 5 feet 5 3/4 inches tall (almost a foot shorter than his son Ted grew to be) and had dark brown hair with blue eyes, and a fair complexion. If he was 21 (and 7/12) in 1904, then he would have been born around June in 1883. This would match the year on his death certificate, and – more or less – the April 5, 1883 date cited there.

Samuel Williams death certificate.

He may have lied about his age, of course, and Ted wrote that "he had run off and joined the Army when he was sixteen and was in the Phillipines (sic) with the Fourteenth Cavalry during the Spanish-American war."[13] The actual Army records are almost certainly correct as to his date of enlistment. If he were 16 in 1904 – though claiming he was 21 – then he would probably have been born in 1888. It would not be at all surprising if he were actually 18 7/12 – instead of three years older, though since 18 was presumably old enough to enlist anyhow, I'm not sure what the point would have been of adding three years. He was probably 21. And he probably was born in 1883 and neither 1895 nor 1886, nor 1885.

The least likely date given for Sam Williams' birth was June 23, 1891. That's the date Ted Williams gave when completing his Officer Data Sheet for the Marine Corps in 1952. If Ted had believed his father was born in 1891, then he would have to have believed the possibility that his father had served in the Philippines when he was 6 years old! Sam would have turned 7 on June 23, 1898 - just eight days before the famous Battle of San Juan Hill.

Later, I learned that the San Diego city census of January 1920 showed Samuel and May Williams living at 933 13th Street, with their son Theodore, aged 1 year, 4 1/2 months. Samuel, the census reported, was 34 and his wife was 27. This would now suggest he was born in 1886. Of course, an 1886 birthdate would have meant he was only 11 or 12 during the Spanish-American War (April - June 1898.) The 1920 census also lends further credence to Ted's birth date being an August one. The same census data states that both of May Williams' parents were born in Mexico and both had Spanish as their native language.

May, Ted and Samuel's sister Alice at 4121 Utah Street, San Diego, probably 1941.

Nephew Ted Williams, though, beginning to ask a few more questions via the Internet, was sent information pursuant to his post on a genealogy forum. The 1900 census of Yonkers, New York stated that Samuel had been born in April 1887, to Nicholas Williams (born October 1862), a barber born in New York, to parents who were themselves both New York-born. Nicholas was listed as head of the household. His wife at that time was Maggie [Margaret Higgins], born in February 1873 in England, to parents both born in England as well. Maggie was just 14 years older than Samuel, who had been Elizabeth's son with Samuel before the couple divorced. She came to the United States in 1892, the census informs us. It also reports that she had been married for 10 years, though only in the US for eight. This might indicate that Nicholas Williams had traveled to England, married Maggie, and then brought her back to the United States a couple of years later. Maggie Williams did bear three children, according to the census, all daughters: Veasey, born in October 1893, Alice, born in March 1895, and Effie, born in January 1899. The family home at 46 Sawmill River Road also housed a boarder, a tailor from Pennsylvania named Charles Nickum (it appears.) Charles was born in June 1878. The spelling of Veasey is but a guess, too, based on the handwritten census records. It looks like it says Veacey, but while SABR genealogist Peter Morris finds no trace of the name Veacey in that era, the name Veasey shows up rarely but occasionally.[14]

Based on all the information available, it appears reasonable to believe that Samuel Stuart Williams was born in April 1887. His mother probably was the Elizabeth Miller he listed on his Social Security application. Even enlisting the assistance of more experienced genealogy researchers, I've yet been able to uncover more.

SAM WILLIAMS, UNITED STATES CAVALRY

If an April 1887 date is correct, Sam Williams was 17 1/2 when he enlisted - the age would fit more with the notion that he'd "run off and joined the Army" than would an age 21 enlistment. The notion that Sam Williams served in the Spanish-American War, though, doesn't hold water. Sam Williams had shown his family photographs of him in uniform and said that he had served with Teddy Roosevelt's old unit. Ted Williams admitted a certain skepticism about claims his father made, and admitted that he wasn't sure this was really true. It was. In a way. Sam Williams never went charging up San Juan Hill with the Rough Riders. That event occurred in 1898. Whatever might have been the dates of his birth, he wouldn't really have been old enough to be leading the charge, or even trailing along behind. But as far as we know he hadn't exactly said that he was with the Rough Riders. He said he was with Teddy Roosevelt's unit. That's a different thing. We have seen that he first enlisted at the end of 1904 – years after the Spanish-American War had been concluded.

A young Samuel Williams (standing) with an unknown army friend.

Sam Williams did admire Teddy Roosevelt, though. It is likely no coincidence that his first born son was given the name "Teddy" – though you never knew what explanation Ted might come up with. In the spring of 1939, he told Harold Kaese of the *Boston Transcript*, "My dad used to be a photographer, until a couple of years ago, when he became a State Inspector of Jails. His best friend was a photographer, too, and when I was born he just naturally called me Ted, that's all."[15]

Ted Williams' original birth certificate reflects the given name "Teddy" – perhaps his birth name was not actually Theodore Samuel Williams. The document says he was born as Teddy Samuel Williams. Johnson and Stout say the name "Theodore" came later, a creation of the Splendid Splinter himself. In *My Turn At Bat*, Ted writes, "The birth certificates (sic) reads 'Teddy Samuel Williams.' I never did like that 'Teddy,' so I always signed my name 'Theodore.'"[16]

As we've seen, the census taker in 1920 also listed the Williams son as "Theodore." By all reports, his mother always called him "Teddy." The census taker may been told that the boy was named "Teddy" but taken the liberty to assume that the youngster was truly named "Theodore" and not "Teddy." Let us revisit this a bit later.

In *My Turn at Bat*, Ted astonishes us, though, by adding, "The 'Samuel' was for my mother's brother, who was killed the last day of World War I."[17]

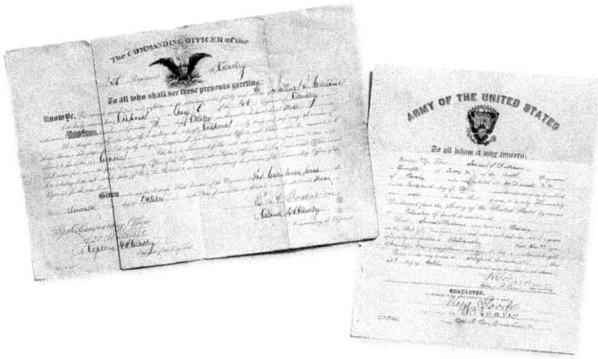

Samuel Williams' United States Army discharge papers.

It never crossed his mind (or John Underwood's?) that the "Samuel" might have derived from his father's name? As it happens, May Williams had a brother who was indeed killed at the very end of the First World War. Her brother was named Daniel, however, and it was Ted's brother who was named after Daniel Venzor.

The United States military records which nephew Ted Williams copied for me provide evidence that Sam Williams was on solid ground when he told Ted that he had served in the military. Samuel S. Williams signed up for a three-year term in the Army of the United States on December 6, 1904 at Yonkers, NY. He was assigned to Troop E of the 14th Cavalry and within just five weeks found himself in the Philippine Islands, arriving there on January 27, 1905. Based at Camp Overton, Mindanao, he was part of the Third Sulu Expedition to Jolo, P.I., serving under Major General Leonard D. Wood from April 22 to May 16, 1905. It was here that he saw combat duty on three occasions.

The Teddy Roosevelt connection presumably comes from Sam Williams having served under General Wood. Wood, later in life the Army Chief of Staff, was commander of the 1st Volunteer Cavalry (the "Rough Riders") during the Spanish American War. His second in command was Theodore Roosevelt. Wood later served as Military Governor of Cuba from 1900-02 and then served in a number of positions, including commander of the Philippines Division.

The Roosevelt connection was thus not necessarily far-fetched. No doubt all the men under Wood's command were well aware that Teddy Roosevelt – who became President of the United States in September 1901 – had served with Wood. There was maybe a little elasticity in the telling, but Samuel Williams did serve in what was at the very least an analogous unit and he did see combat.

The three engagements noted on his military record were all part of the 3rd Sulu Expedition and all took place on the island of Jolo. The first engagement was on May 1 at Maimbung Market on the southern tip of Jolo. Two days later there was another skirmish or engagement at Ipil and then on May 4, he also took part in fighting at Pala's Cotta. He was eventually transferred back Stateside, leaving the Philippines on Oct. 20, 1905 and arriving in San Francisco on November 23, 1905. It remains unclear what he did for the next two years, until his honorable discharge on December 5, 1907, but the discharge papers were signed by a colonel who commanded the Coast Artillery Corps at the Presidio in San Francisco, so it would appear that he may have spent at least the latter period of time serving in San Francisco.

Trumpeter Samuel Williams, like all troopers assigned special skills (for instance, cooks, farriers, or trumpeters), also held regular Army rankings, in his case probably private first class. Other than extra pay for a detail such as playing at a funeral, he shared in all aspects the duties of other troopers – daily horse exercise, stable police, kitchen police, etc., and was considered a regular army cavalry trooper, carrying rifle, sidearm, and (during parade formation) a saber on his saddle.[18] He was promoted to corporal from trumpeter on October 7, 1907 and he also qualified as a sharpshooter in 1907. He held the rank of Corporal at the time of his discharge. The promotion form was signed at Fort Walla Walla, Washington on October 11, 1907, effective the 7th.

Sam Williams was not injured, according to his papers, but as trumpeter he was more likely in the front ranks of any skirmish than in the rear. Attempts to learn more of his actual service from the 14th Cavalry Association have so far proven fruitless. With the passage of time, the likelihood that we will learn substantially more seems slim.

The Sulu Expedition was part of the prolonged battle of the U.S. armed forces against the Moro insurgents. The Moro Insurrection in some respects resembled the war in Vietnam. In both conflicts, the United States became embroiled in battle against an Asian populace which was waging a guerrilla-style war to repel foreign troops. General Leonard Wood was the military governor of the Moro Province from 1903 to 1906. U.S. Army estimates of the number of Filipinos killed in the Moro wars are in the tens of thousands while U.S. fatalities in the 1898-1920 period range from 4,000 to as high as ten times that many. Some have said that as many as 3 million Filipinos may have been killed.[19] A webpage prepared by the National Infantry Museum at Fort Benning describes the Moro Wars in this fashion: "The Moros are Muslim tribespeople who inhabit central and western Mindanao, the second largest island in the Philippines. They have lived there for centuries, quite apart from the rest of the Filipino people, most of whom are Christians. The Spanish, who ruled the islands until 1898 when they were driven out by Americans, had let them follow their age-old way of life and did not try to convert them, but the Americans felt differently. They wanted them to become assimilated, but the Moros resisted with sporadic outbreaks beginning in 1901. In 1903, they attacked American troops stationed near Lake Lanos in the interior of Mindanao. On the nearby island of Jolo in 1906, some 600 rebellious Moros who had taken refuge inside the crater of a large volcano (Mt. Dajo) were killed by U.S. troops under General Leonard Wood (1860-1927). This raised a cry of indignation from the American public. Fighting ceased in 1914 and the Moros continued to practice their religion and traditions in peace." In fact, fighting never entirely ended and there is still an active Moro National Liberation Front active in armed insurrection at the start of the 21st century.

On discharge, it was noted that Corporal Williams' character was "excellent" and that "no objection to his reenlistment is known to exist." His horsemanship was "good." Ted recalled, "I've got pictures of him: a little guy, posing behind a horse that was lying down, getting ready to shoot over the horse, and another of him at attention, standing real straight with a bugle slapped against his side."[20] The photographs probably were among those destroyed when Hurricane Donna devastated Ted's home in the Keys in September 1960. Samuel Williams' discharge papers further note that he had performed "service honest and faithful" and was entitled to a travel allowance. His travel destination on discharge remains unknown.

The next fact I was able to determine is that he somehow wound up at Fort Wingate, New Mexico on October 29, 1908. What he did in the intervening 10 months is unclear, but at the time of this second enlistment, he declared his occupation as "photographer." Whether this is a skill he learned while in the 14th Cavalry or seconded, if such he was, to the Coast Artillery Corps, is unclear. He also may have taken up the trade after discharge, but perhaps failed to make a go of it and chose to re-up for duty again; that would be pure speculation. He joined Troop M of the 5th Cavalry Regiment for another three years. For some reason, he enlisted as a trumpeter again. And he was 25 years, 6 months old, which fits his earlier declaration. He'd either grown 1/4 inch or the measurement was slightly different; he was listed as 5'6" on re-enlistment. He still had blue eyes and dark brown hair, and several scars were noted on various parts of his body, for identification purposes.

When he enlisted this second time, he provided his residence as 27 School Street, Yonkers. When he had enlisted the first time, he indicated that he himself lived at 26 Park Avenue, Yonkers, though his father lived on Neppi-han Avenue, Yonkers. If he had run away from home, he was at least willing to have his father notified in case of emergency. He also signed up right in his hometown, in the enlistment office at 45 Warburton Avenue – not the act of someone covering his tracks. Nonetheless, it may be that once Sam left home, he chose not to return.

This time, his marksmanship rating is hard to determine. A deep crease created by a fold in the papers renders the rating impossible to read. His horsemanship, however, had improved to "excellent." His character was noted as "very good." There is no reason to think this was a downgrade of the previous "excellent" rating. Chances are it simply reflected a differing subjective judgment from the commanding officer. There was "no unauthorized absence of record" and again he had performed "service honest and faithful."

During this term, most notably, he had been transferred from Ft. Wingate to the Hawaiian Islands, arriving January 13, 1909 and apparently serving the full tour of duty there until October 28, 1911 when he was given his discharge papers at the Schofield Barracks by the colonel commanding the 5th Regiment. He was entitled to travel pay, but the form made it clear that he was "not entitled to transportation to U.S. unless claimed within 30 days of discharge." Perhaps they were concerned that he might enjoy it in Hawaii enough to want to stay. More likely, it was simply Army policy. He may well never have used his allowance; while in Hawaii, Sam Williams met and fell in love with a soldier from another army – May Venzor of the Salvation Army.

In an interesting footnote of sorts, some of Ted's relatives in Santa Barbara reported meeting a baggage handler who worked the trains in California and claimed that Ted had a Filipino half brother -- who perhaps even lived in southern California. This well could have been, had Samuel Williams sired a son in The Philippines. Leigh Montville followed up on this lead, and dropped me an e-mail: "I tracked the guy down, all excited, and he said he had heard it from his aunt. He checked with her and said it was all bogus, that his aunt is 91 and suffers dementia...Ah, well...."

There have been other leads as well, some of which remain uncertain. Tom Carmody, who I "met" on a genealogy site, told me of a retired nun in her 80's named Joan Williams. She apparently contacted the Ted Williams Museum and offered to do calligraphy work for the display cases, but it never happened. Tom's mother, Cecilia Williams Carmody is, he says, Ted's first cousin once removed. There is a lot of detail Tom has assembled which makes sense, and a lot that doesn't "compute." Ongoing research may lead to further information.

MAY VENZOR OF THE SALVATION ARMY

May Venzor was serious about dedicating her life to service in the Salvation Army. She was active in the Army from age 12 or 13 and, on her 17th birthday, Corps Cadet May Venzor was given a Bible "by her comrades in the Santa Barbara Corps" on May 8, 1909. 1909? Ted's birth certificate says that she was 25 when Ted was born. This would mean she was born in 1893, or possibly late 1892. If she had been born in 1893, then her 17th birthday would have been 1910. Her obituary, and her gravestone, both show her as having been born in 1891. Yet another confusion of dates! You can't be born in 1891 and be 25 years old when giving birth in 1918. The inscription in the Bible is clearly May 8, 1909, and this would support an 1891 birth date. Ted's birth certificate seems to be misleading. One of those it may have misled was Ted himself. He believed his mother had been born on May 8, 1893, according to information he filed with the Marine Corps in 1952. This is the same form on which Ted had his father born in 1891, though, so should

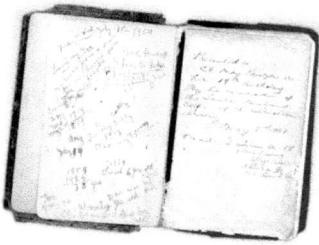

May's bible: how many souls did it save?

perhaps be discounted. Official California death records have May born in 1891 and her sister Mary being born on April 18, 1893; it's extremely unlikely that May was born about three weeks after her sister. Of course, Mary's stated birthdate could have been wrong as well, yet May was well aware of her sister's tragic murder and might have been expected to have commented had the records of the day gotten the year of her sister's birth wrong.

On August 26, 1909, May Venzor entered the training college in Chicago, located at 116 S. Ashland Avenue. Salvation Army National Archive files today indicate that she entered the Salvation Army's Training Home in Chicago "out of the Petaluma, Calif. corps at the age of 19. Her career sheet indicates that she played the guitar, piano, and cornet."[21] A May 8, 1891 birthdate would mean she was 18, not 19, at the time she entered the Training Home.

She graduated January 12, 1911, and was appointed a Lieutenant in the Salvation Army. The diploma also constituted an order to travel, which read in part, "You are appointed

May Williams, young Salvationist.

to assist in the command of Honolulu Oahu, Senior and Junior Corps, So. Pacific Province, and you must please leave for your new appointment on January 20, 1911, without fail."

In Honolulu, she served under D. O. Major Willis. The address of her quarters was at 153 Bieretania [sic] Avenue. On November 27, 1911, when she was promoted to Probationary Captain, she moved from one command to another in Hawaii, and began working with the Senior and Young People's Corps. On January 12, 1912, in effect the first anniversary of her Hawaiian service, she became a full Captain in the Army.

After Sam Williams was discharged from the United States Army in October, 1911, he may well have stayed on Oahu and forfeited his right to paid transportation to the U.S. He'd met May Venzor.

How May became a Salvationist is unclear. Manuel Herrera told me, "May loved to go to church when she was a young girl, and she picked the Salvation Army when she was about twelve or thirteen. She used to go down to the street corner and sing praises of Jesus. Songs. Somebody would come over and say, 'Mr. Venzor, your daughter is down there singing with those Salvation Army nuts again.' He'd go get her and bring her home. Where do you think she was at the next weekend? Back down there." Perhaps the liveliness of Salvation Army revival meetings of the day appealed to young May.[22]

The Boston Globe reported that she first joined the Salvation Army on July 4, 1907.[23]

There is no question that May Venzor (later, Williams) was a dedicated Salvationist and one of the hardest workers they had. She also knew how to work with the system, as the many photographs of her with such public figures as the mayor of San Diego illustrate.

May Venzor in her class at the Chicago Salvation Army Training College.

Yet May seems to have both risen and fallen in the ranks, for one reason or another. After nearly 33 years of service, on March 8, 1944, she held the rank of Envoy and was appointed both Publication Sergeant and Visiting Sergeant of the San Diego Citadel. Starting as a lieutenant in 1911, thirty-three years later, she was just becoming a sergeant?

May Venzor and Samuel S. Williams were married on May 13, 1913 in Santa Barbara, California. The wedding was officiated by Staff-Captain Howard Clifford at the Corps Hall. "The marriage marks the end of her service as an officer," explained Kimberly Mack, an historian with The Salvation Army Museum of the West, because "until very recently officers could only marry officers. To marry a non-officer meant giving up one's rank. Which is not to say she was no longer a soldier or a Salvationist, but rather she gave up working as a pastor."[24]

One can understand that May Venzor gave up quite a lot in marrying Sam Williams. She surrendered her status as an officer in her beloved Salvation Army.

It might not have worked out that way. Sarah Diaz reports that Sam Williams had planned to enter the Salvation Army and make a career, but after training in Honolulu he had a change of heart and left the ranks. Apparently, it was not the right fit. Sarah told me that Sam had run away from home. He was, she said, "a very nice person. He always used to tell us kids that he was a Yankee, from New York. When they fell in love in Honolulu, he had to come to Santa Barbara to ask for her hand."[25]

When the couple was married, May's younger sister Sarah Venzor (later, Diaz) served as the flower girl at their wedding. The Williamses moved to Los Angeles and Sam first found work as a streetcar conductor. It was probably a relatively short stint. They stayed with the Ponce family as they got settled in. Drawing on the craft he had noted on re-enlistment at Fort Wingate, Williams worked as a photographer at the Mitchel [sic] Studio in Los Angeles in 1913 and 1914.

Sometime in 1914, Sam and May moved further south, to San Diego, and Sam began work at the Velour Studio at 820 5th Street in downtown San Diego. Here, Ed Linn says, he "eked out a living of sorts." Ted said his father worked "taking passport pictures and snapshots of sailors and their girls, and he wouldn't get home until nine, ten o'clock."[26] The information that Sam Williams had served as a streetcar conductor came from his sister-in-law Sarah Diaz.

In these happier days, Sam Williams taught May how to color photographs, working to add color to black and white photographs.[27]

I was prepared to try dialing M-2819, the telephone number listed in his 1923 Petition for Degrees to the S. W. Hackett Lodge of Masonic Order in San Diego – but, 80 years later, that number didn't seem to contain enough digits. In the petition, he gave his date of birth as April 5, 1885. I'll forego

A postcard sent from Hawaii by May to her parents, 1911: note the Spanish.

further comment. Williams was elected a Freemason on December 11, 1923 and stayed a Mason throughout his life. On death in 1952, the Alamo Lodge of Walnut Creek paid $10.35 for a floral piece at his November 20, 1952 funeral service. This we know because the Walnut Creek lodge sought reimbursement from the Hackett Lodge.

We will return to more on May Venzor later.

SAM WILLIAMS AND HIS SISTERS

Even if Sam had run away from home, this may not have reflected as much a sense of enmity as a desire to seek adventure and find his place in the world. He did, at least in later years, maintain contact with his three sisters. I found a bit of information about one of those sisters early in 2001. In *My Turn At Bat*, Ted wrote about his uncle, a fireman in Mount Vernon, New York. It was a pretty well-known story, how Ted – frustrated at one point in the 1940 season – popped off to sportswriters about how maybe he'd just give up the whole thing, quit baseball and go and become a fireman like his uncle. Ted's comment, "Nuts to this baseball. I'd sooner be a fireman," received national play. It also prompted opposing players and fans on the road to start blowing sirens, ringing bells and showing up at ballparks in big fireman's hats. So, who was this uncle? Would there be an opportunity to track another branch of the family tree?

Ted gave his uncle's name as John Smith. Wonderful. That seemed like about as difficult a name to trace as any I could imagine. There are indeed people named John Smith, though. I went to Mount Vernon and checked the public library. By looking through fire department files in the city records, I was fairly readily able to locate a John Charles Smith and he was listed as married to Effie Williams, surely Samuel's sister. I was even able to come up with a photograph of the firefighter. After leaving the library, I drove by the apartment where he and Effie lived for many years and where Ted had visited.

Later, I phoned the current Mount Vernon fire chief and was rather efficiently directed to Edward Donovan, retired to New Hampshire but who had served on Engine 6 with Ted's uncle. He remembered John Smith, who had been known in the firehouse as "Beanie" Smith. Donovan remembered well when Ted came to visit and told a colorful anecdote about the young Ted swinging the long fire broom as though it were an elongated baseball bat. "He used to pick up a broom on the back of the fire engine and swing it a little bit," Donovan explained. John Smith drove Engine 6. "That was a great big fire engine. He was good at it...getting the water on. It was an Ahrens-Fox, a great big fire engine. He was the only one who could really handle it. Six. That was the engine company I was on with him. His wife was Effie. She was a Williams. Her brother was the one who worked in photography. That made Ted Williams her nephew. His [Beanie's] badge number was 31. My badge number was 62. I used to say to him, 'You're half of me.'"

May's Salvation Army Captain's Commission, 1911.

John Smith developed bursitis at a relatively young age. "He couldn't drive or wrap up hose on the street," Donovan said, so he took disability and retired. John and Effie moved to Florida. The couple had no children, Donovan told me, and if there's any name more difficult to research than Williams, it is probably John Smith.

Donovan was impressed with Ted's interest in his family. He told me that Ted kept in fairly close touch with his aunt. "I'll tell you one thing about Ted Williams," he said. "When I worked with his uncle, he used to call up and ask how his aunt was. I never forgot that. He made a phone call no matter where he was. Chicago or Detroit, he'd call the firehouse and ask for John C. Smith, and ask how was Aunt Effie doing. I thought that was a nice thing. I don't know if there was a problem with his Aunt Effie but no matter where he was, he'd call up and ask his uncle, 'How's she doing?' I thought that was wonderful, really. You know how busy they are. He called religiously."[28]

So, one of Ted's aunts on his father's side was Effie W. Smith. I learned that Ted's dad had two other sisters by asking the man himself. When I had dinner with Ted Williams at his home on April 28, 2000, I took the opportunity to ask him a few questions about his family. Primarily, I was asking for confirmation of information I'd gathered regarding his mother's side of the family, wanting to learn more about his Uncle Saul Venzor and the role Saul may have had in shaping Teddy's attitude towards baseball.

He didn't offer much about his father's side of the family, except to let me know, "My dad had three sisters. Little bitty gals. Around 5 feet, all of them. He was the only boy. He ran away from home and joined the Cavalry. They got there and they found out when he was in the Cavalry that he was only 16 or something."[29] He didn't mention his sisters by name, and I didn't have the opportunity to follow up because the conversation soon switched to his friends Bob Breitbard and Bobby Knight. Ask Ted a question about his family background and you'd soon find him on another topic, maybe talking about a fish he'd once battled. This is a man who was much more at ease talking about salmon on the Miramichi than about his own family. It had never been a comfortable topic.

There was Effie, yes. Another aunt was actually remarkably easy to find -- after all, her photograph appears in more than one of the books written about Ted. I didn't put it together, though, until Ted had mentioned that he had three aunts on that side of the family. A couple of years later, I saw a photograph with Effie, Alice, and Mae. Was this Mae, or was this May? The photograph is one which nephew Ted Williams owns; he sent a scan of it to me by e-mail. It depicted what I took to be two of Ted's aunts – Effie and

Alice – along with Ted's mother. But on closer inspection, the "Mae" in the photograph's caption was not May Venzor Williams at all. We concluded that this was another May – the third aunt. Another possibility is that it was Minnie Mae Williams, Sam's second wife, but she seems to have been known as Minnie, not Mae. As we will see, the third aunt's name might have been Veasey and not Mae – though perhaps Veasey enjoyed a nickname. It's also possible that the Mae in the photograph was simply a friend and not a relative at all.

John C. Smith, fireman and Ted's uncle.

Attempts to learn more about any of the sisters have so far borne no fruit. Perhaps the sisters did not, either – the general consensus in the family seems to be that none of the three had children. Ben Bradlee, Jr. discovered in Miami Beach a retiree who had known the three sisters. Roselle Romano said that Alice Williams had married Phil Sheridan, a New York City police captain, and the two Sheridans had retired to Miami Beach. In the late 1950s, Effie and John Smith moved down, to a place two houses away from the Sheridans. Veasey, who Romano knew as "Vivian," came down to visit. After her husband (Tom Grey, a machinist with Con Edison) died, she moved to the area herself. Effie died in 1971, Vivian (Veasey) died in 1978, and Alice in 1984. Effie and Vivian were said to have worked as bookkeepers, and Alice as a carpet weaver.[30]

SAM WILLIAMS AND HIS WORK

Sam Williams worked at a number of jobs. As far as we can tell, he never returned to shipbuilding, but certainly he pursued photography throughout his life – and his grandson Ted Williams has also found work as a talented photographer and graphic artist. Sam was also politically connected in some fashion. It's not clear how that began, but Governor Frank Merriam of California was a patron later on.

Samuel Williams was also a United States Marshal. Or at least a deputy United States Marshal. On October 12, 1931, A. C. Sittel, himself a United States Marshal working for the Department of Justice in the Southern District of California, appointed Samuel S. Williams a salaried Deputy U. S. Marshal in place of J. K. Wilson who had resigned effective close of business the day before.

"Mr. Williams was born April 5, 1886," Sittel's letter to the Attorney General in Washington read, "his address is 4121 Utah Street, San Diego, California, his occupation is Professional Photographer; his salary is $1440.00 per annum." His official residence was to remain in San Diego, and "his duties are to be the serving of process and any such work as I might direct." A copy of the Deputy U.S. Marshal's Oath of Office was attached.

Ted Williams and his aunt Alice, left with "Mae," center, and his aunt Effie, right. The woman listed as "Mae" is possibly his third aunt, Veasey (who may have gone by the nickname Mae).

Charles P. Sisson, Assistant Attorney General, wrote back to Marshal Sittel confirming the appointment and his authority to appoint Williams as a Deputy Marshal, grade Caf-2, at the indicated salary.

Merriam served as governor from 1934 to 1939. In 1934, Williams was appointed inspector of prisons for the state of California, Linn writes.[31] During the latter years of his regime, Sam Williams was Chief Jail Inspector of the State of California, until the position lost its funding in 1939 around the time Merriam left office.[32]

Ed Linn speculated that May Williams might have helped her husband link up with the governor. Sam Williams already had his appointment as U. S. Marshal, though, three years before the governor assumed his office. However it came about, the connections seemed to have been significant. When the Bay Bridge spanning San Francisco Bay was opened, Sam Williams was sent an elaborate invitation to the ceremony. He apparently also served for a while as a Sheriff in San Diego.

Sam may have been a bit of a "wanderer" and may have been absent from home a fair amount, but he left some good memories behind with some members of the family.

Samuel Williams.

"Samuel used to drive to Santa Barbara. He loved my dad, and him and my dad used to talk and talk and talk. He gave us a ride in his police car and he even let us push the button for the siren. Aunt May would come over and she'd go to Grandma's. My mother never went a day without going to see my grandma. Every day she'd go see her."[33]

When the marriage between Sam and May fell apart, Sam finally gave up on making a go of it in San Diego and traveled north (apparently with his secretary - Minnie Mae Dickson.) May's sister Sarah told me, "He falls in love with the woman that was supposed to be his secretary. I just happened to run across a little slip where she gets a divorce from Samuel [May]. It just broke her heart because she didn't believe in that. She couldn't imagine anyone, you know: a divorce. She was just heartbroken, but there was nothing she could do. She even went up there and tried to make up with him, with Samuel. No, he had this woman so there was nothing she could do."[34]

At least for a while, Sam seemed to operate out of Sacramento, with an office at 616 K Street. Per at least one extant report to the Governor, Samuel S. Williams served as "Chief Inspector of Jails, State of California." He also seems to have set up a photo studio in San Francisco, at one point.[35] The Walnut Creek studio was named the Williams Photograph Studio and it was located at 1523 Main Street. That address now houses an independent coffee shop of some sort. The telephone number was Walnut Creek 2502 and, intriguingly, his stationery listed "branch phones" Concord 8266 and Lafayette 2153. Did he really have three offices? From what little we know, it seems unlikely. The Williams family household was an exceptionally modest one, according to people who visited May Williams at home, and we do know that Sam Williams had difficulties in business. There are inferences that he may have had trouble with alcohol. Ed Linn writes that, after World War II, Ted received letters from his father "asking for money - like say, six thousand dollars - to open a new photography shop, and then asking for more money after he had blown the six grand on something else."[36]

When Samuel Williams died on November 16, 1952, it was only after a long illness and a prolonged stay in a convalescent home. Ted was in training with the Marines, and apparently at Cherry Point, North Carolina at the time of his father's passing. Though he could certainly have received leave for the funeral of a parent, there is no indication that Ted interrupted his military service to travel to the Bay Area for the ceremony. We can only guess at his reasons. He may have felt that there had been so little contact for so long, and what contact there was may have just seemed like a series of requests for money. Ted wasn't happy about being back in the Marines, either, training for combat at age 34. He may well have just hunkered down and brooded for a couple of days, then got back on with the matters at hand.

INTERLUDE: SAM AND MAY WILLIAMS - STANDING ON PRINCIPLE

Sam Williams

Sam Williams comes across as a bit of a colorless character about whom rather little is known. We do know that he served two stretches in the United States Cavalry and saw combat in the Philippine Islands. He'd been posted in the State of Washington, in New Mexico and in San Francisco. He'd certainly been places and done things. Stationed in the Territory of Hawaii, he met and courted May Venzor, a striking woman whose parents had come to the U.S. from Mexico. He traveled to Santa Barbara to ask for her hand in marriage. His new mother-in-law spoke very little English. We can certainly give Sam Williams credit for breaking the mold a little, and for a degree of adventurousness.

Maybe it wore him out. Ted felt that his father lacked drive. Drive is something May Williams lacked not. Sam may have retreated into a shell, finding himself confronted with a wife that their son Ted later wrote was "religious to the point of being domineering, and so narrow-minded."[37]

Sam Williams may have been a bit retiring, and not often around home, but he did have a profession as a photographer. He also served in law enforcement for much of the 1930s, as an employee of the United States Department of Justice, Deputy United States Marshal of the Southern District of California.

Less than four months after his appointment, we find that Sam Williams participated in a February 1932 raid on illegal alcohol imports from Mexico. Prohibition was still in effect and the Justice Department and San Diego police joined forces to raid some smugglers and confiscate their wares.

Sam Williams stuck with law enforcement into the late 1930s, and in early 1937 was named the State of California's jail inspector. It was a temporary appointment, paying $180 a month. (We can recall that his son Ted had signed with the San Diego Padres baseball team in June 1936 for $150 per month.) The appointment was made pending civil service examinations in April 1937. Williams "won a top position in civil service ratings and became the permanent inspector in October, 1937." [38]

In the course of his work, Williams attended the American Prison Association's 68th annual congress in St. Paul, Minnesota in October 1938. His son had just completed his Triple Crown season for the American Association Minneapolis Millers ball team, the season having ended just three weeks before Sam Williams came to town. Ted was in the area, barnstorming in Minnesota and North Dakota, but it's unknown whether father and son met at the time.

Left to right: Samuel Williams, Chief H. H. Scott, Arthur A. Jones,
with confiscated contraband, February 1, 1932.

Chief Jail Inspector Samuel S. Williams submitted a report on October 14, 1938 to Governor Merriam and the members of the State Social Welfare Board. The four-page report detailed his October 2-7 visit to the APA Congress. He was there as a representative of the California State Social Welfare Board and the State Department of Social Welfare. During the Congress, he took out membership in the APA and participated in the formation of the affiliate National Jail Association. The meeting brought together hundreds of interested parties, from federal officers, wardens, sheriffs, jail inspectors, and chiefs of police to welfare workers, church officials, the governors of many states, and...Salvation Army officials. Accompanying Mr. Williams were the warden of the U. S. Penitentiary at Alcatraz and the Superintendent of the California Institution for Women at Tehachapi.

While in St. Paul, Williams was given a tour of the Ramsey County Jail by the sheriff of Ramsey County, former heavyweight champion of the world Tommy Gibbons. "A fine and efficient sheriff," was Williams' assessment. One might suspect that the starring season Ted Williams had just completed cropped up in conversation with Sheriff Gibbons or St. Paul Police Chief Clinton A. Hackett.

Williams also met Director James V. Bennett of the Bureau of Prisons, Washington, D.C. and presented his executive assistant with a report he had conveyed for Sheriff Biscailuz of Los Angeles County.

A wide array of topics was addressed at the Congress, and Mr. Williams reports attending 17 meetings. He said he was asked many questions about jail inspection procedures in California, and that many looked favorably on the "watchful eye" method employed in California. It was, all in all, the reasonably typical, and well-organized report of a competent government official. Inspired by his participation in the proceedings, Samuel Williams concluded that he would work "with renewed and refreshed efforts for the improvement of the jails in California, and for more and more progress in reclaiming for useful lives the offenders against our laws."

Though there is always work to be done, Williams expressed, "From what I learned California is keeping pace with the best jail program at the present time, in line with the foremost states, New Jersey and Virginia."[39]

At least for a period of time, Sam Williams was part of the law enforcement establishment. He lost his position the following year. On July 12, 1939, the Fresno newspaper reported, "California's only jail inspector, Sam Williams, a former deputy United States marshal from San Diego, today found himself out of a job."

There had been a mix-up involving the state legislature, the attorney general's office, the department of social welfare and other bodies. The news report stated that the elimination of his job was because the 1937 legislature had "failed to include the statute providing for a state jail inspector." Williams had been operating on a temporary appointment since early 1937, while the omission was rectified. He took the civil service examinations in April 1937 and was named permanent inspector in October 1937, and all seemed well until the 1939 legislature met.

Senator Ray W. Hays of Fresno was a member of the senate's governmental efficiency committee, which killed the bill making provision for an inspector of jails in California. His argument was that the position would be duplicative of existing services that could be provided by the various counties. County health departments and other agencies had "ample authority to make jail inspections." Whether they ever did, or did not, might be another matter. The *Fresno Bee & Republican* informed us that Williams, "while acting as state jail inspector, made several inspections of the many times condemned Fresno County Jail, his last in connection with a grand jury inspection and has made repeated recommendations for correction of the crowded conditions in the jail."

Reading between the lines, it may not be a coincidence that the senator from Fresno on the committee was the one who killed the bill authorizing the position of state jail inspector. It seems safe to conclude that, at least to some degree, Sam Williams' efforts to fulfill the mandate of his position came up against political opposition in Fresno and resulted in him losing his job.

Sam Williams next turns up in San Francisco, resuming his profession as a photographer, later moving to Walnut Creek where he and his second wife ran a photographic studio until his death. It wasn't an easy existence. There were times he turned to his son for financial assistance. One newspaper report said he had been "semi-indigent."

Sam Williams died at the San Ramon Rest Home on November 16, 1952. His son Ted already held four batting titles and was in the Marine Corps receiving his final training as a jet pilot. Sam's second wife survived him by 25 years. Perhaps the most fulfilling period of Samuel Williams' life was in 1938-1939. He had moved to northern California and felt he was doing good work for the State of California, he had a son beginning a career in major-league baseball, and -- it is only speculation -- he may have at least taken some degree in pride at having lost his position only because he was pursuing his profession so diligently.

May Williams

May Williams was willing to stand up for principle, too, even at personal cost. We have seen that May Venzor married Sam Williams, though it cost her officer status within the Salvation Army. Marrying outside officers' ranks caused her to be "busted" down to a private in the service.

May's dedication to the cause was remarkable. She didn't hesitate to go into barrooms or Mexican jails, to pursue collections or to right a wrong. Alice Psaute, a younger friend and fellow Salvationist, remembers going to the Coliseum in downtown San Diego. "That's where they had fights. They called them prize fights. Boxing matches. It was so smoky in there it was hard to find your way around in the place. May was there. She sold our magazine and went into bars and took collection. She would go tavern collecting."[40] Ted had written, "She would campaign right down into the seamiest sections of San Diego, and across the border into Tijuana, going into jails to minister to people and even into the red light districts if she thought she could get a contribution." [41]

Manuel Herrera offered a bit more insight into May's character. "She never argued. May was a very innocent type person. Naive, kind of, and yet when they gave her a direction of something to do, boy, she was going to do it. There was no two ways about it. She was very direct with the Lord. There was nothing going to stop her, and she loved to be around men. She loved to entertain men, to catch their attention. She didn't care where she was at.

I used to worry about her as a kid. I guess I was about 12 or 13 and we'd go down and see her. We slept on the floor, which was no problem. She had a little home down there on Utah Street. We'd take her downtown and leave her there. I say, 'Mom, is she all right?' And Mom would say, 'Oh yes, this is her job. Seven days a week.' I'd say, 'Where are you going, Aunt May?' and she'd say, 'I'm going to see the Devil.' She'd take her Bible and her Salvation Army *War Cry* and she'd head right for the Marines in the bar. There was no stopping that woman. She was really well known in San Diego."[42]

It didn't bother her to go out in the street and praise the Lord, Manuel wrote. "She was the Angel of Tijuana. Do you know why she was named that? Here's what happened. I asked her. I went down and I said, 'Aunt May, can I see you?' She said, 'Come on in' - she was laying in bed. My mother had told me the same story and I got the same answer. Here's what May told me. I said, 'How did you become the Angel of Tijuana?' She says, 'Well, I used to go down to Tijuana to help the unfortunate people and I was walking by the jail. Some kids were yelling to me, 'Hey, lady. Hey, lady, can you help me?' and I looked up and I said, 'What's wrong?' 'They put us in jail. These people put us in jail.' She says, 'Did you do anything bad?' They said, 'No.' She says, 'Are you Christian people?' 'Yes.' 'I'll get you out of here.'

May Williams (standing with guitar and glasses) with the Salvation Army Band, Tijuana, Mexico.
"I got permission to go to Tijuana, Mexico to hold open air meetings."

"So she went inside the jail and wanted to speak to the commandant. They're all wondering what this little old lady is coming in there for. They're looking at her and she was saying, 'I would like to talk to the commandant. I have something to say.' She went up to him, and she says, 'In the name of God, Jesus Christ, those American children are not to be in there.'

"They went back and forth. He explained her this and she told him – in the Bible – she started pointing out Scripture to him. He took her down there and they showed him where they were at. She says, 'The rats wouldn't even live in there.' It was filthy. It was beyond reproach. And they opened the door and he says, 'Open the door and let's let them out.' He did. He opened the darned door and she took the kids home. They were probably 13 or 14. They were American kids. I don't know what transpired, but after that, when people found out about what she did, somebody tagged her the 'Angel of Tijuana.'"[43]

The "Salvation lassie" set records for selling *War Cry*, the publication of the Salvation Army. In time, according to clippings from Salvation Army publications, May sold well over 100,000 copies of the magazine.

By the time she was in San Diego, though, she'd lost the officer status she'd earned coming out of the training college. In February 1934, May Williams was "publications sergeant" and also "in charge of the county jail meeting conducted in the women's side." Back in 1913, when she married, she had given up her officer's rank. A captain at the beginning of 1912, she was reduced in rank as a result of her marriage in 1913.

She was still but a sergeant by 1934. She "married out," as the saying went -- married a non-officer. She knew in advance what the consequences were, but she married for love. Perhaps she felt secure in her sense of mission and realized that the calling was more important than the rank. She could still do good work as a soldier.

Alice Psaute says, "We're getting more progressive, after one hundred or some years. In those days, they were very strict. And if they thought you had an interest in a person of the opposite sex, they'd automatically station you as far apart as possible, so we had some bad marriages that happened because of things like that." [44]

Sam Williams proved a lost cause, however, and no doubt May learned this early on. Her sons, though, were another matter. She could still raise them in the Army. Teddy was "dedicated," but the lure of baseball proved too powerful. He used to attend Sunday school, no doubt reading *The Young Soldier*, the Army's Sunday school publication of the era. Alma Parton was his teacher. But when he started playing baseball, he stopped going to Sunday school. Sunday was the big day for baseball on the playgrounds. "I guess the dedication didn't take," Ted wrote. "The thing was I had to go so damn often. I just hated it."[45]

We also know how mortified Ted was at the ribbing he received from school-mates, who would tease him about being dragged along with his mother when she was on the street with the Salvation Army band. Ted was embar-rassed that his mother was "Always gone. The house dirty all the time." He said he was "embarrassed about my home, embarrassed that I never had quite as good clothes as some of the kids, embarrassed that my mother was out in the middle of the damn street all the time."[46] Ted told Bobby Doerr that when his mother brought him along with the Army band, "I used to try to get behind the big bass drum so that I could hide."[47]

San Diego Mayor Harley Knox and May Williams, with copies of the *War Cry*.

Ted may also, in time, have come to blame the Army for taking his mother away from the family. His parents drifted apart, but it wasn't as though one or the other of them stayed at home with Ted and his younger brother Danny. They were both out working in the evenings. While this freed up Ted to spend more time hitting baseballs, Danny had no such compel-ling drive. And Ted noticed. May sometimes

spent more time at 830 8th Avenue, Corps headquarters, than at home at
4121 Utah Street.

Alice Psaute acknowledged, "I think maybe he felt that if his mother wasn't
spending all her time down there, maybe his brother would have turned
out a little better." As Alice points out, "That was not the Salvation Army's
fault. It was probably her fault. After you go there a long time, you get very
dedicated and you go every day whether you're supposed to or not."[48] If you
truly believe you're doing the work of the Lord, then the idea of a day off can
seem, to the True Believer, almost like sacrilege.

It seems safe to say that Ted did fault the Army for its impact on his family.
He put it so bluntly and succinctly in *My Turn At Bat* that on a quick read,
one could overlook five words about family, and the depth of sentiment and
resentment revealed therein. Consider the second of these two sentences:
"My mother was strictly Salvation Army. As a result, strictly non-family."[49]

Ted's friend Frank Cushing was willing to give May the benefit of the doubt.
"She neglected her own sons. What I think was that she was so sure in her
own mind that she meant only the best that she couldn't see what she was
doing to them."[50] Ted filled the void with his baseball, and his fishing, and
he was fortunate to find a number of other families who treated him as their
own son. Danny was not so lucky, and he acted out in response. He rebelled
against rules and expectations, falling in with a bad crowd, but his wayward
ways may have been built right into him. A few years after Danny died of
leukemia at age 39, Ted wrote of his younger brother, "Some guys have absolutely no respect for authority, and Danny was one of them."[51]

On August 21, 1932, Evangeline Booth, the Commander of The Salvation
Army in America, and the daughter of founder General William Booth,
appeared at the Hollywood Bowl. This was an important event. While there
is no record that May Williams took her sons – Teddy almost 14 and Danny
just recently 12 – to L.A., there's a very good chance that she did. She was a
loyal soldier in the Army of the Lord.

There came a time, however, when May Williams stood up to the Army leadership. It was in February, 1936. She had attained the rank of envoy and already earned perhaps a more meaningful status – May Williams was already known as the "Angel of Tijuana" to the readers of the *San Diego Sun* and throughout the city. When she protested a new Salvation Army policy regarding the treatment of transient indigents, she was stripped of her rank by Major J. L. Kelso and reduced to the rank of private.

A dramatically-told story in the pages of the *Sun* illustrates the effect this new policy had:

> On the door of the Salvation Army headquarters at 830 Eighth Ave., is a crude sign. It reads: "Indigent men applying for relief, come back at 9 p.m. Applications received at no other time."
>
> A man in shabby clothes went back a few minutes before 9 p.m. A small sedan was parked near the front of the door. It contained two men.
>
> The man in the shabby clothes hesitated, and while he waited, a second poorly dressed individual shuffled up to the Army headquarters and stepped inside for his evening meal.
>
> The men in the parked auto remained sitting.
>
> It must have been a slim meal, for he remained inside only three minutes. Then he wandered off down the street, stopping momentarily to glance down into a gutter in search of a cigaret butt.
>
> He had hardly passed out of sight when four youths, cold, hungry and obviously tired, stepped up to the Army door. They didn't have a chance to enter.
>
> The two men who had been sitting in the darkened auto in front of the headquarters, clambered out and accosted the youths. A few words passed, and then the youths were directed to "climb in -- you're going to the police station."
>
> Maj. Kelso stood in the doorway as the youths were driven away. He didn't see the other figure, however, the man who first had approached the Army headquarters in search of a warm meal.
>
> The man had melted away into the shadows after seeing what had befallen the four youths.
>
> Maj. Kelso stood in the doorway for more than a half hour -- but no more hungry men came for aid. The word must have gone out that it was "unhealthy" to go there for food any more.[52]

Envoy May Williams objected to what she termed the creation of a "trap." Homeless men were told to arrive at 9 p.m. but police prowl cars awaited them, "backed up to the curb ready to take the applicants to central station for examination." The men were reportedly "required to pass police fingerprint examinations and were subjected to 'third degree' tests." When she spoke up, Kelso stripped her of her rank. Private Williams' demotion sparked protest from the Mayor of San Diego, Percy J. Benbough. May was, the *San Diego Union* reported, "lovingly known throughout the city as the 'Salvation Army lassie'" and was "well known all over San Diego." The mayor announced that he was sending a letter to the commanding officer of the Salvation Army in Los Angeles and that it would be signed "by a number of prominent citizens who have expressed surprise at the army's action in dismissing Mrs. Williams, a beloved member of our community. We will ask that a full investigation be made on this matter. Mrs. Williams has endeared herself to the entire community, and we should like to know why the local command has summarily dismissed her." The mayor's language was blistering. "You might as well have the police cars come to church services evenings and compel those who attend to submit themselves to police surveillance. Unfortunates who attend the Salvation Army services and later apply for aid have found that the police are on hand to 'shake them down.' Any habitual criminal, of course, would not apply to the Salvation Army for aid. I understand that Mrs. Williams was dismissed because she objected to this practice."[53]

An editorial in the *Sun* allowed that the internal affairs of the Salvation Army are its own business, but noted that "to thousands of San Diegans, rich and poor, Mrs. Williams IS the Salvation Army. The jingle of her tambourine is welcome music in most of the restaurants and dine-dance places of San Diego and Tijuana. Her kindly smile and her quiet helpfulness are known to untold thousands who have lived here. The paper urged looking into the conditions May Williams had decried. "Is the city, through the police department, over-stepping its authority by herding homeless transients into the city jail for no reason at all except that they are transients and homeless? If that is the case then the alliance between the city and the Salvation Army's shelter must be terminated." The paper urged that the Salvation Army not make a mistake which will "mar" its "splendid reputation."[54]

Ted's nephew Ted Williams has done some family research, too, and he is the one who first talked with Alice Psaute. May survived the controversy, of course, but it helped that her winning ways had impressed city figures in high places. "Only pressure from the mayor got her reinstated, if not at full rank. 'I won't give the Salvation Army another dime or eat another donut without May Williams.'" The mayor threatening not to eat those Salvation Army donuts may have made the difference.[55]

Anita Rasmussen, a year behind Ted at Hoover High and a young Salvationist, was "assigned May's downtown 'beat'" and she told the *Union*'s Joe Hamelin that May's demotion really cost the cause. "She knew all the people in all the right places, and a lot of people in the wrong places, too. She had access to the major, the chief of police, business leaders...and she would go into the red light district, there was white slavery in those days, and minister there as well...I remember asking the head of the gas and electric company for a donation, and his telling me, 'the day they reassign May Williams, that's the day I'll support the Salvation Army again."[56]

Psaute remembered the brouhaha nearly 70 years afterward. "She protested something I would have protested, too. It was the Census Board -- it sounds sort of like the Senseless Board -- that was the board that is sort of in charge of who could be a solider and if they have to do any disciplining. My mother was on that board, but she was still very good friends with May. It didn't affect their friendship at all."[57]

The discipline also did not shake May's faith. First a captain, then a sergeant, now a private, she continued to sell *War Cry* and hold outdoor gatherings. Like Ted, she may have been a little loud at times. "She had a good open-air voice," Psaute remembers. The scrapbook that Psaute's mother kept contains a few clippings from later years as well. In May 1943, May Williams was named to head the Christmas Kettle Campaign – in charge of the traditional Salvation Army kettles we still see today at Christmas time. The funds collected were to aid 900 underprivileged San Diego families.

In December 1949, the *San Diego Union* informed readers that May Williams had assumed the responsibility of selling 18,000 copies of the special Christmas issue of *War Cry*. Though 1949 was the year Ted came in second to George Kell for the American League batting title by .0001557, his mother may well have won the title for selling the largest number of publications in the country. A clipping from a Salvation Army newsletter reads that she "at one time held the record for *War Cry* selling in the entire United States." [58]

May Williams was blessed to have such faith. She never lost her faith, and in that she was blessed as well.

MINNIE MAE WILLIAMS, SAM WILLIAMS' SECOND WIFE (MARCH 2, 1897 - OCTOBER 9, 1977)

Minnie Mae Williams (note that middle name) was born March 2, 1897 in Oakville, Iowa to Joseph Henry Dickson and Effie Emma Johnston (note that first name) on March 2, 1895. She first arrived in California in 1937, give or take a few months.

Sam Williams and Minnie moved north to San Francisco, living at 328 West Portal, but moved to Oakland (based on his membership in the Scottish Rite based in Oakland), and by 1947 to Walnut Creek, where they lived on Hillgrade Avenue. Samuel Williams was a Freemason, and belonged to the S.W. Hackett Lodge #574, the Oakland Scottish Rite and to the 14th Calvary Association in Santa Monica, CA.

Minnie had been Sam's secretary at one point. It's unclear when they actually married. In 1942, she worked at Tidewater Associated Oil in the city. She was apparently a photographer herself, since on her funeral record (according to information supplied by her sister, Mrs. Lou Alexander of Fort Worth, Texas) she was a photographer and had been one for 20 years.

Does this mean she had taken it up five years after Sam died? She outlived him by 25 years. It's hard to know. She was listed as self-employed. How successful she was is also unknown; she is not listed in the Yellow Pages or Contra Costa County telephone directories in those years. She had moved to another home on Danville Boulevard, and died after a stay in the San Marco Convalescent Hospital, at age 82 on October 9, 1977.

Minnie Williams was a member of the Christian Science church, and worshiped at First Church of Christ Scientist in Walnut Creek. Interestingly, Sam Williams had first married a Salvationist and then a Christian Scientist. Attempts to locate others in Minnie Dickson Williams' family have so far proved fruitless. Minnie herself is remembered by a few in Walnut Creek, including a boy to whom she gave a Ted Williams signed baseball, one she had had around the house.

Larry Frank was about 13 and he had a 1959 Fleer baseball card of Ted Williams. His mother Mickie used to take Minnie home after church. When Minnie found out that Larry had this card, she asked to borrow the card to photograph it as a memento. When Larry came by her house to pick it up, she noted his passion for baseball and gave him a baseball, telling him "This is my last autographed ball." As he got a bit older, Frank pitched briefly for Arizona State. More than 25 years later, Larry Frank is assistant baseball coach at a high school in St. Louis and for the past seven years has thrown batting practice for the St. Louis Cardinals before home games. "It inspires me to look at that baseball," he says.[59]

Her death certificate lists her as having been a self-employed photographer for twenty years, which would suggest that she took it up five years after Sam Williams died. Her sister Mrs. Lou Alexander of Fort Worth, Texas, no longer lives at the address provided. Brother Dwight Dickson no longer lives in Sedalia, Missouri, either.

When Samuel Williams applied for his Social Security card on March 1, 1940, he indicated that he was still married to May Venzor, and that his parents' names were Nickolas (sic) Williams and Elizabeth Miller. Most accounts say that May and Sam divorced in 1939, despite a last appeal by May to work things out. In any event, by the time Minnie Mae applied for hers, in October 1942, she and Sam Williams were married.

Enough on Ted's stepmother, though. He seems to have had some contact with her, but certainly it was not much. It is noteworthy that he had maintained contact for at least 20 years after his father had died.

Let's go back and look at Ted's mother in a bit more detail.

MAY VENZOR WILLIAMS

Who was May Venzor that Samuel Williams married?

Ted's birth certificate does suggest that his mother was born in El Paso in 1893, but it could be that she was actually born in San Diego. San Diego, Texas, that is. Sarah Diaz had told Manuel Herrera that her older sister May was indeed born in San Diego, Texas. He questioned this, naturally, but she reaffirmed it. He'd never heard of San Diego, Texas before. It's not the sort of name anyone would come up with on their own, a small town of 1,500 people at the time, the county seat of Duval County. The County Clerk of San Diego, Texas, however, shows no births at all registered with the surname Venzor. (There is no record of her birth in El Paso, either.) Her gravestone in the Goleta, California cemetery indicates that she was born in 1891. The California Death Index reports her birth as May 8, 1891 and death on August 27, 1961. We will assume the 1891 date, in part because we do know that her sister Mary was born in April 1893.

May may also have been born in Mexico. That's what she said when completing her application for a marriage license in 1913.

Sarah was quite adamant on the geography, though, Manuel wrote me. "Sarah told me that May Venzor was born in San Diego, Texas. I said, 'No, Mom, you mean San Diego, California!' She looked at me like I was lost and said, 'If you look on the map, you will see a San Diego, Texas, just to the left of Corpus Christi.' So, I pull out our trusty map and sure enough I find San Diego, Texas right on highway 44 and near highway 359. Yeah, the old gal was correct! I am 150 percent [certain] that Aunt May was born in San Diego, Texas."[60]

May's parents emigrated to the United States from Mexico late in the 19th century. Ted's maternal grandparents were Natalia Hernandez and Pablo Venzor. The family was Basque in origin and had settled around El Parral

(Hidalgo del Parral) near the border of Durango in the state of Chihuahua, Mexico. Nephew Ted Williams and I enjoyed visiting the area in July 2010.

The United States of Mexico, like the United States of America, is very much a nation of immigrants. Though Mexican by nationality, Sarah Diaz was concerned to present the family as Basque ("Basco"), not as Mexican. Racial, ethnic, and class differentiation is seemingly of concern in every culture and many people will try to draw distinctions which portray them as superior in some fashion to those around them. In Mexico, those who claim pure European ancestry have long held themselves to be superior to the "Indios" – the indigenous people. One infers that Sarah didn't want to be seen as a lowly "Mexican" but to accord herself and her family the more prestigious European background. It's as though the family just passed through Mexico on its way from the Pyrenees to the United States – and that may well have been true. "We have no Mexican heritage in our family," she told me, "although my father and mother were in Mexico. We are Basque." Admitting that there is no written history to document the family history, she also wanted to let me know early on that, "I have an uncle who was the administrator to the governor of the state of Chihuahua."

As Sarah understands matters, and here she does admit the possibility of some indigenous blood in the family, the Basques came to Mexico "during

May and her son Ted, during a World War II visit.

the war when the English sent Maximilian to try to take over Mexico. So the French came, and they were the Basques from the Pyrenees between France and Spain. When they came to war, naturally they were looking for young girls. These girls, they were pregnant from the soldiers and from the Basques. When the war was over, they took off and went back home and left the girls with the child. These children that were born, they didn't have a name to say, 'He was my father' or 'My name was So-and-so.' We have no way of knowing the real history."

Sarah said that her uncle, who served as this administrator in Chihuahua, told her that he had fallen in love with one of her mother's sisters and they'd married. Sarah's mother was Natalia Venzor (1869-1954), born a Hernandez. Natalia's mother -- Ted Williams' great-grandmother -- was Catarina R. Hernandez (1837-1931). Sarah described her as "very fair. Blue eyes, blonde. In our family, we go back to where we're very fair, light-complected and with blond hair."[61] Catarina Hernandez was a Rubio.

Archduke Ferdinand Maximilian set sail from Europe for Mexico in April 1864, where he became – at least briefly – the Emperor of Mexico. Other hopefuls from France and Spain may have come with him, or around the same time. It could well have been that the Venzors and the others in the family had only arrived in Mexico some 24 years before Natalia Hernandez married Pablo Venzor.

It could also have been much earlier. The Center for Basque Studies of the University of Nevada in Reno notes in a report from a 1994 conference in Jalapa on the Basques in Mexico, "From 1795 to 1810 in Valladolid, Michoacan, there were more than two hundred Basques involved in the church, government, commerce, ranching, mines, and sugar factories." The report details many other communities throughout Mexico where Basques were noted.

A tangent:
ERNESTO PONCE AND HIS SISTERS CONSUELA AND RUTH

Though Sarah could not recall the name of her uncle the administrator during our interview, my visit in 2000 with Ernesto Ponce in El Paso made it clear that the uncle was Federico Ponce, who came from Valle de Allende, Chihuahua. Ponce was an administrator on the staff of Don Luis Terrazas, the "cattle baron of the world" who operated out of the governor's place in Chihuahua, Chihuahua. Federico Ponce was related to the Her-

Left to right: Natalia H. Venzor, May Venzor, Catarina R. Hernandez with baby Chester Amidon, Sarah's son, 1926.

nandezes through marriage; he married Eulalia Hernandez, one of Natalia's sisters. Natalia (and Eulalia) had other siblings: a sister named Micaela (nicknamed May) and another named Eduviges and brothers Manuel, Rayo, Cristofal and Santiago.

Rayo Hernandez (August 12, 1874 - January 8, 1968) was quite a character. He and Manuel Hernandez lived in Santa Barbara. Cristofal Hernandez lived in Los Angeles and Santiago Hernandez in Bellflower. Rayo was a big man who managed ranches in the Goleta area. He told Sarah Diaz that "Pancho Villa wanted him to ride with his band of warriors. He came to Santa Barbara with two pearl handle 45's and his Stetson hat." [62]

Manuel Herrera, named after Rayo's brother Manuel, continues, "He [Rayo] was different than the rest of the brothers, he was very manly and proud. He always wore that Stetson hat and was very powerful in his manner. He lived to be about 99 years old and was very alert before he died. I used to offer him a ride when he was waiting for a bus, but he usually refused because he wanted to look at the girl who rode the bus too. He was a very positive man and had a build like a stud horse."

Ted almost certainly knew many of the Hernandez family, since quite a few of them lived in and around Santa Barbara and would have attended family gatherings, especially when May and family would visit from San Diego. Santiago Hernandez, in fact, worked on Santa Barbara's Spaulding Ranch, according to Ernie Ponce's wife Mary (born Maria Mercedes Serrano.) Further reinforcing the Basque connection, Mary mentioned that her mother's name was Llaguno, and that both of her parents were Basque. [63]

Ernest Ponce knew the Hernandez family in El Parral. "El Parral, in Chihuahua, was where my mother and father met. It's a little town. My mother used to tell us that there were no schools in those days. The parents would let their children work for people who were educated – they would babysit and take care of their children, so that they could be taught and learn to read and write."[64]

Natalia Hernandez, before she married Pablo Venzor, "didn't like living out like that" and consequently did not learn how to write, though she did learn to read. "She could interpret the American paper," Sarah told me. "In later years, she could understand every word, but she wasn't able to speak [English] and she wasn't able to write. We finally taught her how to write her name."[65]

Federico Ponce, though, was highly regarded by Don Luis Terrazas. Impressed with the young man, Don Luis sent him to North Adams, Massachusetts (a Bliss Business College was located there at the time) where he studied accounting. On his return, he reportedly became chief accountant to the cattle baron. Years later, Ted Williams would make the trek to Boston as well, to pursue another profession.

One thing neither Ernest nor Mary Ponce thought to mention during my visit was that Ernest also had two living sisters. Two aunts of Ted's -- Consuela and Ruth. I only found this out over two years later. Mary had mentioned that she had some photographs tucked away in a box from their honeymoon to Santa Barbara and San Diego – where they stayed with Sam Williams for a week. (May was away, and they didn't recall why but they never met her – perhaps she was on a Salvation Army retreat?) Every six months or so, I called Mary but she was often not feeling well and I wasn't able to motivate her to seek them out. Finally on almost the second anniversary of my visit, I realized (in going over my notes) that they

Rayo Hernandez with his second wife, Lupe.

had a son and a daughter living in El Paso still. So I phoned Wayne Ponce to see if perhaps he could help his mother locate the photographs, were she still willing to share them. I had to leave a voice mail for him the first time I called, but when I called back maybe 10 days later, he'd spoken with his mother and urged me to call her so she could give me the names, address, and telephone numbers of her two sisters-in-law who both lived in the Los Angeles area.

I called a few days later. But I was on the road – visiting Ted Williams in Oaklandas it happens – and had not brought the phone cord that connects my handheld cassette recorder with the phone. This was around 7 a.m. on November 22, 2002. Should I change my flight plans and head to Los Angeles instead of home to Boston? After all, one of the sisters was 92 and the other was no spring chicken.

I did not change my plans, but once home again I did telephone Connie Matthews (born Consuela Ponce) on November 26 and talked with her at length, following up with more questions on December 10. The next time I was in Los Angeles, in February 2003, I had the pleasure of meeting Ruth Gonzales at her home in Norwalk. They were not aunts of Ted, they both explained. They were first cousins to May Venzor, and cousins to Ted.

Juana H. Molina with her sister, Natalia H. Venzor.

The Ponces' mother was Eulalia Hernandez and her sister was May Venzor's mother. [The more common Basque spelling is Eulali.] In my understanding of genealogy, this means that Ernesto Ponce was really Ted Williams' second cousin, not his uncle. But perhaps we are splitting hairs. In many cultures, including the Hispanic culture along the US-Mexican border, the terms *tio* (uncle) and *tia* (aunt) are used as much honorifically and as a mark of familial respect than their precise genealogical definition might suggest. In this sense, as a somewhat older close relative, Ernesto Ponce was Ted's *tio*, his uncle.

Connie was eight years older than Ted, but remembered several visits to San Diego in the 1920s. She confirmed everything that Ernest had told me, but also told me something that I hadn't learned before – May Venzor's given first name was Micaela. May was a nickname. Connie told me, "Now his mother, May, she was my first cousin. May was really Micaela, but you know everybody called her May. Micaela was her real name." It seemed as though it was a name that ran in the family, since Micaela was also the name of one of Natalia's sisters. Thus, May was named after her Aunt Micaela or Mikaela. Mikaela is a reasonably common Basque name.

Connie shared a couple of nice memories of Ted Williams as a carefree kid: "When Ted was little...he must have been 7 or 8 years old, we were there in San Diego. We were there for about a week, my sister Carmen and I forget whether it was Ernest or Fred who drove. We were coming to Santa Barbara and we stopped in San Diego on Utah Street - I remember where they lived on Utah Street. Micaela was always with her hat. I still remember she wore a Salvation Army hat and sold that *War Cry*, that paper. She'd go out to stand in town, selling the paper – that *War Cry* paper – and I remember Ted – Danny was younger – they'd wrestle like crazy. Sam, her husband, had the photo shop, but the kids, we'd take them to the beach. They were on vacation.

"I remember Ted [another] time that we visited in San Diego. He must have been about 10 or 12 years old and we took him to the beach, you know. After he grew up and became famous, he really went to the East Coast.

"Ted would run after me with crabs. He'd pick them up with his hand from the shallow water there at the beach and chase the heck out of me, after me with a crab. I was just terrified with those animals. But he was a nice kid. That's all I remember. He was just a regular kid and so was Danny."[66]

The Williams family was perhaps a happier family in those days. Connie remembers more: "Actually, Micaela, we saw her then but I didn't pay too much attention. She was very nice. We had real nice dinners. I remember she had a real nice German maid in San Diego when we visited, and that woman when we come back from the beach or wherever, we would run all over, she baked the best fish – I'll never forget – and the best salads. Especially grated – I'll never forget the grated carrot salads that she made. It was a German maid that she had."

Perhaps before the Depression hit, the young family was better off and could afford the services of a maid or housekeeper.

I asked: was that Natalia, or was it Micaela? "It was Micaela. She was working, so she hired this German maid while we were there. Maybe she was there before we came. The two kids were real nice. They were regular kids, you know. Just like kids. They were always running here or running there. Sam was too busy. I never did visit his shop.

"We had a girl that we'd take over and this girl had some kind of a tic in her eye. She would wink, automatically wink. I guess it was some kind of a problem she had with her eye. She was just a friend of Carmen and Carmen had invited her over one time there when we were visiting May. Sam, I remember at the dinner table, says, 'Hey, Rose, quit winking at me. I'm a married man, you know!' He was very outgoing. I liked him. He was very nice to us all the time we were there."[67]

Mary Ponce also remembers Sam Williams as a good host. She told me, "When we got married in 1936, we went on our honeymoon to California to visit all the relatives because they were all the way from San Diego to Santa Barbara. We stayed at Sam Williams' home. May was a Salvation Army captain and she never was at home. We stayed with Sam for two weeks on Utah Street. We stayed there and Sam would get up every morning and cook a wonderful breakfast. He cooked everything -- hot cakes, waffles, scrambled eggs, fried eggs, turnovers, muffins, biscuits. He was a marvelous cook. He cooked for us all the time we were there. Sam was a lovely man. He was so nice to us."[68]

I came across several people who had favorable impressions of Sam Williams. We may not have a rich picture of him today, but he apparently had his charm and was no doubt more than the one-dimensional person we sometimes find depicted in the books on Ted Williams, where he just comes across as remote, pretty uninterested in his son's baseball playing, and as a father away from home a lot.

There was some visiting back and forth between El Paso and Santa Barbara. Connie's sister Ruth Gonzalez remembers Maria Cordero (May's sister Mary Venzor) coming to visit El Paso at one point, but she also recalls that when her mother and father visited the Williams home in San Diego, "nobody was ever home." Two other Ponce siblings, Fred and Ruth's twin sister Elvira, visited Santa Barbara in 1939 and from that visit we have a photograph which includes May and Danny Williams on the beach. One of Ruth's memories of the Williams boys was not the best – but we're talking five-year-olds here. Ruth, born like Ted in 1918, still recalls visiting Santa Barbara in 1923. Both Ted and Danny set on her and Elvira and started roughhousing and choking them. At that moment, they wanted nothing more than to get away from Ted Williams and his little brother Danny.

Ted's brother Danny suffers from some of the same uni-dimensionality. Before we dig into Danny a little more, though, let's try to learn more about mother May's family background. That is, more or less, where I started this deeper quest into Ted's Hispanic heritage.

PABLO & NATALIA VENZOR, TED'S GRANDPARENTS

Pablo Venzor (1868 - November 29, 1920)

Natalia H. Venzor (December 1, 1869 - January 2, 1954)

As we have learned, the family emigrated from Mexico to the United States. We don't know how long the Venzors and Hernandezes had lived in Mexico, but it wasn't a place they felt they could stay. A settled life in Mexico seemed impossible, as the winds of change were beginning to blow across the northern states of Mexico.

Pablo Venzor learned a trade, Sarah explained. "When they married, my father -- golly, my mother was just a young woman. My father was very well trained. He had a good trade. He was a bricklayer and a stone mason."[69] Pablo and Natalia married in 1888. "My father used to tell my mother, 'Now remember, three eights' -- trying to explain to her the numbers." Natalia and Pablo Venzor had one child in Mexico -- Pedro Venzor was born the year after they were married, in 1889.

Maybe Pancho Villa wanted Rayo Hernandez to ride with him, but Villa posed a threat in the minds of others. "When Pancho Villa was going wild in Mexico, taking over the towns and what have you, the Mexican people called him a 'Robin Hood' because he used to take from the rich and give to the poor," Sarah Diaz said. Many others fled northern Mexico, and crossed the border.

As political troubles began to brew in Mexico, though, the young couple decided to join what was becoming an exodus north to Texas. The Venzors left much earlier than the Ponces. In fact, Ernest was born on the floor of the governor's palace in Chihuahua on July 25, 1913. "Right there on the floor," says Ernie's wife Mary. "As soon as she [Ernesto's mother] could walk, they fled. They kept on, hiding in the sage and all the bushes and stuff until they got to the border. He was four months old when they crossed the border. It took four months to get from Chihuahua city to Juarez, to cross the border. In those times, everybody crossed the border."[70]

The path to the north from Chihuahua was typically through Juarez, and then across the Rio Grande to El Paso. May Venzor was born in El Paso in 1891, it seems -- though if the San Diego, Texas story is correct, it may be that the family passed through El Paso but then continued on to the valley in south Texas in search of work. One way or another, they did pass through El Paso, and ultimately made their way west to Santa Barbara, California,

Left to right: Rose (a friend), Elvira Ponce, Helen Hansen (Danny's first wife), May, and Danny Williams. Mission Beach, San Diego, 1939.

arriving, according to a notation on the back of a family photograph, on June 24, 1907. There is a suggestion that there may have been a couple of uncles who had already settled in California. I didn't get a chance to follow up fully with Sarah Diaz to learn more about what might have prompted the continued migration, from Texas on to California. No one I've asked since seems to know, but it wouldn't have been atypical for some family members to have followed other relatives who may have settled in Santa Barbara and then let the family in Texas know that they found better prospects on the West Coast.

There were a lot of uncles in the Hernandez family. "My grandma [Catarina] had 14 children. Fourteen children. When she married my grandfather, her first pregnancy she had twins, but one died at birth. After that, she had 13. The last pregnancy, she had twins again. One of them passed away. I didn't know some of my uncles. They stayed in Texas."71 But some had gone ahead to California and Pablo Venzor, with his growing family, followed.

What the family did in El Paso from, more or less, 1890 to 1907 is unclear. We do know that some of the family had achieved a degree of prosperity in El Paso. David Ronquillo, a lawyer in San Diego (all references to San Diego will be to the city in California unless otherwise noted) today, and a relative of Ted's (his mother Lilia Molina and Ted's mother were first cousins) had a

Pablo Venzor with children, left to right: Pete, May, Mary, Maria (an orphan), and Daniel, El Paso 1903.

grandfather who was a relatively well-to-do dairyman in El Paso. He also had the water rights for Fort Bliss, Texas, which provided another good source of revenue.

Ronquillo's *abuelo* was convinced to come to California by a relative, a Senor Calderon who was a pastor. In their case, it was a later migration, sometime in the 1920s. "We're told that he sends green grass blades back to my grandfather to convince him that he should come west. So finally he convinces him that he should come west. I guess it's a caravan of Model T's that they drive out here. All six kids remaining with the family, plus their belongings.

"So they come all the way out, and they have a big tent meeting in Chino. It's during that tent meeting that all seven children are called to the ministry. All the women are called to be missionaries, and the two men are called to be pastors. One man, Federico, was my uncle. Geno's grandfather. He follows his calling to the ministry."[72] David introduces another element here, that of the strain of evangelism in the larger family. There were many in the family who felt called in one way or another.

Geno Lucero is another relative of Ted's, a musician. His Aunt Mary and David's mother Lilia both became missionary companions in Nogales, Mexico, and it's David's understanding that they spent three or four years working there. David Ronquillo adds, "They were all very involved with the Free Methodist Church. My mother was a missionary with May and worked with her in San Diego. She wasn't in the Salvation Army. I'm not sure how May got in the Salvation Army. That was never explained to me, but I do know that Geno's grandfather -- my Uncle Fred -- he was in the Free Methodist Church, and I do know that he and May Williams developed together an orphanage in Tecate, Mexico."

Perhaps typically Basque, the family was very independent. Natalia Venzor was a Baptist and devoted to the Mexican Baptist Church in Santa Barbara. Santa Barbara at the time was "99 percent Catholic" and the Venzors were in the minority. Some of the children were "put down" by some of the Catholic kids as a result. Some of that independence may have served them well, and strengthened the faith of those who truly believed.[73]

Geno added, "My grandfather [Federico Hernandez Molina] and Ted's mom were very, very close, because my grandfather was a pastor. His name was Fred. He was a Hernandez. He had a church in San Diego, about the time I was born and after. 1949. He used to help May with a lot of stuff because she was always helping the poor people, especially down in Baja. Tijuana and stuff. And so my grandfather, in church, would collect stuff for her, for the Salvation Army. It was a Free Methodist church. So it was basically pretty close to the Salvation Army's doctrine."[74] Geno's aunt Esther Slagle confirms the working relationship, and then introduces yet another unexpected twist: "There's a big discussion in the family between Basque [background] and Russian. In our side of the family, there's a lot of talk about there being a Russian colony in Mexico. My aunt used to say that the men wore big tall boots and white smocks, and that they had big long beards. They must have spoken a different language, living in the middle of Mexico. I guess as time went on...my one aunt thought it was Russian. I have a cousin who went to Russia and she brought back all these pictures and it was like looking in a mirror. That would be the Hernandez side. I understand that Rubio is from Portugal, which would make me think more Basque. They say it's a Portuguese name."[75]

Some of the professions the men followed are ones that one might associate with a Basque background. There were shepherds and stonemasons, and dairymen. "Santa Barbara was a cow town," remembers Connie Matthews. "Before Santa Barbara changed, before these guys built all the beautiful hotels and all that. It was nothing but a little old town. Manuel [Hernandez] had a dairy called the Sisters Dairy, because there were eight sisters and five brothers. They all ran the dairy and would deliver the milk in a little old wagon with a little horse. In the 1930s, can you imagine? The beach was wide open and it was never like Santa Barbara is today." 76

Mr. Venzor apparently used to take the family out to the country and ride in the old wagon for a visit. "Well, on one trip," Manuel Herrera wrote me, "the weather got very foggy as it often does on the coast and they unknowingly got lost. The horse stopped and wouldn't go a step farther and Mr. Venzor was getting upset because of his stubborn horse that was pulling the old wagon and would not budge an inch. So the old man got out and took a look. Hell, they were at the edge of a cliff and if the horse took three more steps, over they would go into the gully. The old horse had some common sense. A smart horse, huh? I heard that story every time we looked at the old wagon picture that was taken in 1920 at Santa Barbara."[77]

Manuel, in the same e-mail told another story. "You will like this story. Grandmother Natalia went down to visit May in San Diego and the kids [Teddy and Danny] were still little. Well, the boys had a dog and they used to fight over the poor pet. If one had the dog, then the other one wanted it in his room. Soon they were in the middle of the living room fighting over the poor dog with not a stitch of clothing on. Natalia was embarrassed and didn't know what to do; they were mad and paid no attention to her requests. They both wanted that dog and nothing was going to stop them, not even their grandmother Natalia."

Ruth Gonzales describes her: "Tia Natalia was a sweet lady. She had golden honey brown hair. She would buy rolling papers and roll her own cigarettes. She would crumble cigars and smoke that." And she remembers when Natalia came through El Paso with her sister Eduviges or their way to Europe, where Natalia was headed to visit her son Daniel's gravesite.[78]

Pablo Venzor was able to put his talents as a stonemason to good effect. "He built a lot of buildings and bridges in Montecito – that's a very restrictive area of our very famous Santa Barbara." Manuel tells about coming home from the cemetery, visiting his grave with Sarah Diaz. "We would go into Montecito and drive along the main road and there would be a sudden stop by a bridge. Mom would show us the bridges he built in that area. I guess she was sentimental and wanted to share her father's works. Beautifully made of sandstone, a local rock, and granite shipped in from other parts of the state. There was an arch on both sides, really strong looking with abutments at both ends. I told her that the bridge had weathered many storms and that it must have been built correctly. Yes, was her remark, my father built that bridge and many more of the old ones here in Montecito and Santa Barbara. The sandstone bridges are a work of art."[79]

Sarah added her memories: "My uncles were all very well trained in a trade. They were bricklayers and stonemasons and they did a lot of work here. Then they started dairies here in Santa Barbara. They were good milkers. And good sheep-herders, but they'd have to go to the island. At that time, they had a lot of sheep there. My father was a sheep-herder. He used to go to Santa Cruz Island here in Santa Barbara, in our channel, and he used to shear sheep. He used to have to do it by hand."[80]

On the way to Goleta, Pablo and Natalia Venzor with Paul, Bruno and Jeanne.

Natalia and Pablo had nine children who reached maturity. Two others died in childbirth. The offspring they raised, and their children and their children's children are an incredibly colorful and challenging family, ranging from working cowboys to shepherds and stevedores, to cement truck drivers and beauty shop operators, and to baseball stars and evangelists.

One area they never really got involved in was politics, though Ted Williams made several campaign appearances and recorded messages of support for Republican candidates, even including a local candidate for sheriff in Massachusetts in the 1990s. Ted was a lifelong Republican, following in his father's footsteps – Sam Williams was at least somewhat friendly with Governor Frank Merriam of California, as we have seen.

After arriving in the United States, Pablo Venzor started off as a Democrat, but one day in El Paso became a Republican. He found himself at a Republican rally and, according to family lore, you could get yourself a free beer by signing onto the Republican rolls. Pablo had more than one beer, but only signed up once.

Ted Williams never truly knew his grandfather, who died around the time Teddy was two years old, but family lore says that when he came to visit, he liked his grandfather so much that he wanted to sleep in the same bed with him. They had a hard time convincing Teddy it wouldn't be right, but he insisted until he finally gave in to his mother.

In the early days of the film industry, Santa Barbara was a bit of a Hollywood outpost. In the first decade of the twentieth century, the city had developed good rail and road connections to other communities up and down the California coast. A number of westerns and other films were shot at the old Flying A Studio which was right downtown on West Mission Street between Fifth and Chapala. The American Film Manufacturing Company set up shop in Santa Barbara in July 1912, establishing themselves on the site of an old ostrich farm. The studio, known as the Flying A, was one of the largest studios in the country. Before too long, the studio had even organized a company baseball team as part of the Motion Picture League, which "consisted of teams from different studios in Southern California who played each other as well as local community teams."[81] Until the devastating June 1925 earthquake hit Santa Barbara, the studio was quite an active one.

Sarah Diaz told me of an aunt and an uncle of her mother's. "They were all fair, blue-eyed. You wouldn't think they had any Spanish blood or Mexican blood or whatever in them. They came to Santa Barbara; they used to come and visit us and right away they'd get a job in the moving pictures. That was when the Flying A was right here in Santa Barbara, with Mary Pickford and Mary Miles Mander and William Russell. All those movie stars. We used to go watch them make pictures."[82]

Manuel Herrera told me that his grandfather Pablo Venzor picked up a little extra cash from time to time, serving as an extra in films, but he was cast as a peon every single time and eventually he became angry about the stereotyping, quit on the spot one day, and simply refused future roles.

Pablo's health began to fail, and his son Daniel was taking care of the family until he was called off to service in World War I. Pablo Venzor died in 1920. The family never knew exactly what he died from, but after Pablo was gone, Natalia never remarried. She said she didn't want anyone else telling her children what to do, so she remained single for the rest of her life and took pride in her decision.

"I have no idea when Pablo was born, but Natalia died in 1954 and she was about 84 years old. She should have been born about 1869 or 1870. She suffered from a heart attack and had trouble breathing as well. The last time she was taken to the hospital, she stated in Spanish, "I know I will never return to my home." She had tears in her eyes and we all were crying, I remember that sad day as if it were yesterday! She never came home, she passed away in January of 1954. A sad day in my life."[83]

She bore a lot, but she held the family together as best she could. When Natalia Venzor died, the family lost its center.

Natalia Hernandez Venzor.

In another e-mail, Manuel describes Natalia as "the silent ruler of the home" and he notes that her children, several of whom struggled with alcoholism, "had the common decency to not be abusive in her presence. Since she was a proud woman, I could often sense the hurt on her brow with the drinking and unhappiness." No one in the family would ever curse around Natalia. She was particularly proud of May and Sarah. Her daughter Mary was also involved in charitable works and when son Bruno informed Natalia that Mary had been killed by her son-in-law, she is said to have fallen to the floor and wept, and continued to do so for days.

Natalia was the matriarch, and she held to the old values. Her brothers Rayo and Federico would come to visit, but when they did, they would always announce themselves and ask for the lady of the house - their sister. "As a child I was taught to honor my peers and to listen and be respectful. Rayo, Federico, May, Pete and a few others [impressed me favorably.] Rayo was a giant of a man and when he spoke you listened. The man could do just about anything because he was a rancher in Mexico, as [was] Pete. Heck, those guys could butcher a cow, goat, lamb or what was to your liking to grace the table. I had the best cheese at Rayo's place. He was a real rancher and knew his skills well and the same with Pete. I learned from the older people and, yes, I did respect them just as I did Pete, who was as hardworking a man as I ever knew."[84]

Ted's grandmother would have been shocked to hear Ted Williams express himself, the way he sometimes did. Ted was a master of profanity, and he certainly didn't pick up that way of speaking from his mother or grandmother. No matter how bad off some of her children became with drink, they were never offensive in her presence. She was aware of some of the dysfunctionality around her, though. "Since she was a proud woman, I could often sense the hurt on her brow with the drinking and unhappiness was brought by her sons and one daughter."[85]

"As for Ted and his cussing, I think it came from the guys whom he played with in his young days. He was always playing with older guys and in semi-professional leagues and he must have gotten it from the game of baseball at a young age. He was very much impressed with the old guys, but his Mom never cussed but one time that I knew the gal. My brother Paul teased her and wouldn't stop and she was very upset, he was provoking her and I told Paul to stop, but he continued and she told him off, I didn't blame her at all. My brother was upsetting the old gal and she wasn't well. I finally got him to stop because I was worried that May would have a heart attack. May was not one to cuss and she was not a gossip column like the rest of the family."[86]

Natalia was a mother or grandmother figure to a number of non-family members as well. Manuel remembers something he witnessed as a 6-year-old boy. He relates how a Superior Court judge named Atwell Westwick, senior judge of Santa Barbara, pulled up to Natalia Venzor's house in a police car. The judge asked if he could come in the house and, when inside, asked if he could sit down. Natalia said, "Sure, you're a guest here." She says, "Atwell, did you have the siren going when you came up the street?" He says, "Yes, I did" and she says, "Don't do that. It disturbs the neighbors." This was a man she knew well. It turns out that she had babysat him years earlier.

Manuel shook his head in wonderment. "Here's a man that I later found out put people to death, put them in prison for life -- if you're wrong, he's going to punish you -- and he's over here apologizing for using the siren. She said, 'Atwell, have you been drinking?' and he says, 'Yes.' 'Would you please put your bottle on the table and refrain from continuing?' He said, 'My wife, and you know her, she's divorcing me, and I came here to reminisce and to be consoled.' She said, 'You're always welcome here.' He got on his hands and knees and cried in her lap, for about five minutes. The way he talked Spanish -- he had learned it from her. 'Well, we all go through some hard times; we all have some bad things' and she patted him like a little kid. Rubbed his back. The same thing as she used to do to me. He's crying and I said, 'Man, this guy really loves this woman to come over here and talk to her.'"

Judge Westwick had a home in Rattlesnake Canyon, behind the old mission. Manuel, Sarah, and Natalia all took him back home. On top of the mountain, it was a house like Manuel had never seen before. He saw lights through the fog and said, "Grandma, look, we're in Heaven. Those are angels." Natalia said, "No, *mi'ijo*. That's fog and those are the lamps from the streets." Westwick loved her so much, Manuel said, that "when he had his hardest time, he came to her and just cried."[87]

In some way or other, there were a number of people who Natalia had looked after. Manuel Herrera told me that Natalia had "raised Percy Heckendorff, a very well known lawyer in the area." Heckendorff apparently helped Ted's brother Danny get out of a very serious scrape later in life. It was a case Ted never knew about, Manuel says, and it was never conclusive. Manuel heard Sarah Diaz tell the story several times. "It seems Danny had come up to visit the family from San Diego. He had given a young girl (18 or 19) a ride. We guessed that he met her on the way to Santa Barbara. The next day the police came to the door of the old 1008 Chino Street house and asked to see Danny. They asked if he had picked up a young girl and they described her appearance. Danny agreed that he had and then the police told him that he was charged with rape. The young girl said Danny Williams had raped her, so he was taken away to jail to be charged and arraigned by the local judge.

Heckendorff had been a great friend to the family and now he was hired to clear this matter up. Mrs. Venzor had to mortgage the 1008 Chino Street house so they could get enough money to afford the lawyer and incidental costs. "Well, old Percy was a sharp character. He did some investigating and found a loophole in the security of the evidence. The office where the evidence was stored or secured was not locked and this fact was presented to the judge during the trail. Percy brought the unlocked door issue up to the judge and he said, 'the evidence was not secured, so case dismissed.' Danny was released and the mortgage was returned to Mrs. Natalia Venzor."[88]

Natalia Venzor did have the chance to see her grandson Ted play in major league baseball. Manuel accompanied Natalia to the game. "I remember the only game I saw Ted and the Sox play, at Wrigley Field in Los Angeles. My Natalia was at the game, too! She saw Ted park one out and she winked at me when the ball had gone over the fence."[89] Natalia H. Venzor died early in January, 1954.

Ted attended his grandmother Natalia's funeral and made an impression on his cousin Kathleen, one of Manuel Herrera's sisters. Kathleen told me, "I remember seeing him at the wake, then going to my Aunt Sarah's house on Chino Street in Santa Barbara for a family gathering, where I decided to sit on the sofa beside him and introduce myself. He was very attentive, asked me how we were related, said he was pleased to meet me (which made my head really swell with pride.) I found him to be quite the opposite of what I had heard about him (which was that he could be extremely rude and obnoxious to people.) Actually, he was pleasant, beautifully dressed (style has always been a barometer with me), very slender, and had a definite presence about him. I really liked him. Of course I mentioned that I really loved baseball (which I didn't, but thought mentioning such would gain me some points) and he said to call him for tickets whenever I was in the area and wanted to see a game. I almost asked him for his autograph, but didn't think the timing was right (being my great grandmother's funeral and all)."[90]

Manuel talks about his grandmother Natalia with the deepest respect. She was, Manuel says, "the silent backbone of the family...the quiet hero and leader of the family."

Let us return once again to learn more about May Venzor.

May Venzor Williams (May 8, 1891 - August 27, 1961)

May, who may well have been named after Micaela Hernandez, married Samuel Williams, as we know. She gave birth to four children, though the first two died at birth. Her two surviving children were both boys: Teddy Samuel Williams and Daniel Arthur Williams. Teddy was born on August 30, 1918 – or was he? Again, the birth certificate seemingly raises more questions than it answers. The date on Ted's birth certificate had been changed. Let's revisit his birth certificate once more, this time in some detail. As mentioned before, note also the dating of the physician's certificate: 8/21.

Adding to the confusion is the fact that there are TWO birth certificates. Or more. One is typed and that one has been reprinted in a couple of books, such as page 2 of Dick Johnson and Glenn Stout's book. There is also a handwritten one; it raises still more questions. A handwritten certificate was perhaps completed first, from information supplied by one or both parents, and then a typed copy was completed for filing purposes. The date on the typed one was clearly originally entered as August 20 but has been over-written to read August 30. Yet it was still dated as signed by the physician Steade on August 21.

There are actually two different handwritten certificates, and an affidavit filed by Mrs. Samuel S. Williams. The child's name on what seems to be the original handwritten certificate was Teddy Samuel Williams. It shows the date of birth as August 20. A copy supplied by the Assessor/Recorder/County Clerk of the County of San Diego in September 2004 bears a rubber stamp indicating that the certificate was amended on June 9, 1920.

The county clerk's office also produced an affidavit "for correction of a record" dated May 27, 1920. The affiant was Mrs. Samuel S. Williams and she filed the document which states: The child's name should be given as "Theodore Samuel Williams," and the date of birth as "August 30, 1918." The May 27 date shows us that the affidavit was

Danny Williams in his car with his first wife, Helen Hansen.

filed just shy of eight weeks before Ted's brother Danny was born. Why the pregnant May Williams moved to correct Ted's birth certificate at this time is unknown. The original certificate was stamped "Amended" on June 9, 1920.

At this point – apparently – a new handwritten certificate was created. This one produces the "full name of child" as "Theodore Samuel Williams" but whoever was completing the form seems to have at first forgotten to also change the date from 20 to 30, then compensated for his or her error by over-writing the 20 and making it into a 30. The certificate of the attending physician, though, was not corrected and still reads as 8/21. It was not Ted himself who changed his name; it was clearly his mother who did so when he was less than two years old. But even her attempt to correct the record was botched, leaving later researchers still scratching their heads.

In any event, Ted's birthday was always celebrated on August 30. We've seen that his high school record bears the August 30 date, and May's own hand-written notes to herself sometimes included notes such as "Aug 30 My Teddy 1918." An unidentified clipping from a 1938 Minneapolis newspaper found in the Les Cassie scrapbook at Hoover High reads, "If you like Ted Williams' rhythm at the plate you ought to see him in front of a radio...Ted's a nut on swing bands, rates Benny Goodman tops, but can't dance a lick, says he'll learn this winter...Ted likes Minneapolis so well he's entertaining the idea of getting a job here for the off-season...Williams...received a birthday cake celebrating his twentieth birthday from his mother, Aug. 30, although baseball records say he won't be 20 until Oct. 30...Think what power Ted'll get in back of those homers when he fills out that wiry frame of his."

Ted's official military record also cites August 30 as his birthdate.

Ted was known as Teddy, and even close friends like Dom DiMaggio called him that to Ted's dying day. In school days, though, at least for a while, he was called "T. Samuel" and that got into print at least once in the Hoover High *Cardinal*. The official high school file has his name recorded as Ted S. Williams.

May Williams with baby Ted.

Then there is Theodore Francis Williams. Somehow, someone in Minneapolis seems to have gotten the notion that Ted's middle name was Francis. During 1938, when Ted spent the season playing for the Minneapolis Millers, any number of articles appeared in the local papers dubbing him "Theodore Francis Williams." The middle name stuck for a while in 1939, and occasionally appeared in some of the Boston papers as well. Ted's 1940 Play Ball baseball card issued by Gum, Inc., shows his name as Theodore Francis Williams. Someone figured it out before too long, though. The 1941 Play Ball card had him as Theodore Samuel Williams, and so he remained ever after. It took a little longer to correct his birthdate, at least when it came to baseball cards. The October 30 date was perpetuated from card to card, year to year. The first baseball card to reflect the August 30 birthdate was Ted's Topps card in 1956, his third year with Topps.

Early on with Boston, in the spring of 1938 and again in '39, "The Kid" had another nickname: his teammates and others called him "California."

How do we know that there were two earlier children before Teddy was born? The birth certificate asks "Number of children born to this mother, including present birth." The number "3" was entered. That was question #19. Question 20 asks, "Number of children of this mother still living" and there the completed form reads "1" – Ted. So Ted actually had two older siblings, who had died in childbirth or infancy? That was the conclusion one would draw. I asked Ted himself about this and he said he hadn't known that. Sarah Diaz had, though. She told Manuel Herrera this on several occasions. Both were born before Teddy. Manuel's supposition is that "May kept on working when she should have taken care of herself during her pregnancy."

Another intriguing item: May believed she was doing God's work, but was she really so innocent that she believed herself to have conceived immaculately? I asked Manuel Herrera if he'd ever heard that May might have suffered the loss of two children before Ted was born. "Yes," he wrote me back. "Since you brought that up, it is correct. Mom told me about the loss Aunt May suffered – a child or two at birth. It did occur but, as tradition was in the old days, people never spoke about loss of a child, or loss by sickness of a child at a young age. Aunt May always professed that she had no idea how she got with child and that only the doctor was the one who informed her of the up-and-coming birth of Teddy. She stated, 'In God's name, I have no idea as to how I came with birth?' I always just smiled at her innocent statement! Who was I to doubt her word?"[91]

May was often considered somewhat of a "*santa*" – a saint. But immaculate conception would be going too far.

She did do some wonderful things for people. One family she knew, related to the Rubio family, moved to Los Angeles. May and this family would visit each other, and on one visit she noticed that their daughter, the little girl, had crossed eyes. She told the mother that she was going to take this little girl out. She didn't say what she had in mind. May took the little girl to an eye doctor who worked on her and then May brought her back home, with her face bandaged. "There's blood coming out of the bandages," Manuel told me. "They're all bloody. There's other fluids coming out of the child's eyes. 'Oh my God, May! What have you done? In the name of God, what have you done to our child?' 'Everything's fine.' 'No! Get out of here! We're upset. We can't handle this. This is not right.' May

Ted's handwritten birth certificate.

said, 'Take the bandages off in a week.' 'May, look at the blood! Something's wrong!'

"They took the bandages off in a week. The little girl's eyes were all right. The next time May came over, they got on their knees and apologized to her. I'll tell you, though, May never asked for praise. May never...she always had another job to do. 'Who's next?' was the name of her life, and nothing was going to stop her."[92]

May suffered at the end of her life, but she bore the awareness of her decline with faith and dignity. Sometime in 1954 or '55, "she was in a bus and had an accident. The bus stopped quickly and she was jerked forward. From then on, her back began giving her problems and she began to lean over. That began a real degeneration of her body. It really caused a lot of pain. She was bent over forward. But, you know, in her last years -- she spent a year and nine months with us [staying at 1008 Chino Street with Sarah and Arnold Diaz] -- that woman never complained. She knew she was dying. She never said a bad thing, never gave up her love for Jesus Christ and what she believed in."[93]

Over the years, before she was relocated to Santa Barbara, the house in Utah Street had begun to become more and more cluttered. Ted Williams, the nephew, recalls stacks and stacks of old newspapers piled up around the house, and papers everywhere, many of which were covered with May's jottings – short prayers or expressions of love for her boys.

Ted was kept abreast of her condition, but never visited in his mother's last two years. "He phoned and left messages for her," Manuel remembers. "He didn't come at all. I thought he might, but he didn't. I think it bothered him to see his mother so bad off. He couldn't handle it." Like many people, Ted was conflicted in his feelings about his mother. In his autobiography, he wrote that he was closer to his mother than to his father, but at the same time, her behavior rankled and he found her hard to take. "The last statement I got from Teddy about his mother was, 'My father should have gotten the Medal of Honor for putting up with that s.o.b.', then he slammed his coffee cup on the dining room table and madly walked out the dining room."[94]

Manuel admired the way May dealt with her final days. "This woman was so bad off that she used to put Absorbine, Jr. on herself, and five blankets to keep warm. She had hardening of the arteries and she had several mini-strokes. I'll tell you what, when it came time to go to church, boy, she'd get brand-spanking dressed up. I have never seen a person so committed and so strong-willed about her convictions. It amazed me. To this day, when I get upset and something bothers me, I think about May.

"People would come around and they all loved to be around her. She had an aura of love for what she believed in. She didn't care about the jealousy and everything. I asked her, I said, 'You know, people are jealous of you.' She said, 'In the Bible, it says that people will test you but the Lord will protect you.' She didn't let them bother her. It was never a problem for her. Me? Everything, hell, bothers me."[95]

As a side note, Danny's birth certificate lists his mother's occupation as Salvation Army worker; Ted's listed her as housewife. The work had perhaps become more of a vocation by the time Danny was born, two years later.

May Venzor Williams was a very special woman. When one first reads of Ted and Danny sitting at home at 9:30 or 10 at night, waiting for their mother or father to come back home, one wants to reproach May for not being a good mother. Our historic culture tends to exempt Sam Williams a bit, but only if one subscribes to the double standard that sees the wife as the homemaker.

May Williams with Sarah Adams.

85

The two boys turned out very differently, and many would feel that Ted made the most of the opportunity – befriending other families, but primarily devoting himself to the pursuit of the science and art of hitting a baseball – while Danny suffered the consequences of a breaking home and a "double A personality" older brother. Did baseball benefit because May was a bad mother?

Frank Cushing doesn't think so. He believed that "even if his mother was sitting home all day long, he still would have been down at North Park playground having Rod Luscomb throw baseballs at him 12 hours a day. There were some people who feel she was neglectful, but it wouldn't have made any difference. Ted would have been down at the playground from sunup to sundown. He was totally preoccupied with hitting a baseball. I've never seen anyone with the dogged drive to become the best. It's not just an ego thing. It's a drive."[96]

Of course, there's the question of the chicken and the egg in all of this. "The one thing his mother did show him was total commitment. That commitment took over as far as hitting."[97]

Baby Danny Williams.

If Ted's mother was merely "sitting home all day long," would Ted have been as driven? We can never know.

She was, if nothing else, committed.

Some of the criticism she received rubbed friends the wrong way. One of Ted's Hoover High teammates, Del Ballinger, reacted, "She wasn't out doing bad. She was out doing good. I loved her." "We all did," chimed in Cushing. "May was a wonderful woman. Her calling was that strong religious thing, and she collected money and was extremely good to poor people; it's really hard to knock May Williams."[98]

This was also a woman of courage. It took "guts" to preach in the red light district of San Diego, Manuel Herrera said. "I can remember her telling me as I questioned her while we stood in front of the El Cortez Hotel, 'Manuel, I am taking the word of God to the depths of Sin' and she was pointing to the bars where the Marines and Navy guys were having a few drinks. So much damn guts! Few people have the nerve to serve the Lord like my Aunt May."[99] No evangelist has it easy, confronting people in public places when they would often prefer to be left alone. Ridicule would often result, but Manuel quotes the Bible as saying, "A great many will mock you, but stay fast with the Lord." Chances are he heard that from May Williams.

San Diego writer Barry Lorge heard how May would "trade on her son's name" to raise a little extra for the cause. A bank teller named Mel Powers told Lorge that she'd come into the bank and convince "everyone to put whatever coins they could into her tambourine…She would then canvass the bars along University Avenue, telling patrons, 'I'm Ted Williams' mother. Empty your pockets.'"[100] Not everyone knew the name Ted Williams. An amusing story told to Don Freeman of the *Union* is worth recounting. "One day Mother came home from a downtown shopping trip and told Pop that a very nice lady had been seated next to her on the bus. Mother said that this lady wore 'some kind of a Salvation Army uniform.' So, my mother related, they began to chat. As Mother recalled the moment, this woman suddenly, for no reason that Mother could figure out, said to her, 'My son is Ted Williams!' Hearing this, Mother smiled and said, 'That's nice. My sons' names are James and Charles and Hughie Lyons.' I don't think Pop ever stopped laughing at that one."[101] She sometimes went too far. Joe Villarino recalls that Ted's mother "used to ride the old streetcars and get people cornered on the Salvation Army deal. They'd say, 'Let's go! Off the car!' Ted didn't like that too well."[102]

May didn't let food get in the way of her service. She was the Mother Teresa of San Diego and often skipped meals because of her determination and dedication to the Cause. When she did sit down to eat with the family, there was sometimes quite a pause between seating and eating. "May could pray a supper prayer like no one I have ever met. You could expect a 20 minute prayer and Mom [Sarah] would tell her, 'May, please. Let's eat. We need to eat!' That cut things short, maybe only another 10 minutes. My blood sugar level would drop like crazy, but May never missed a beat with her prayers."[103]

She was dedicated even by Salvation Army standards. She aged early from giving of herself to others, but she left no stone unturned. "There aren't any like her left in the Old Army," wrote Manuel Herrera, "and that is why I don't attend any more. She was a Tough Act to follow, and so is The Kid. My Aunt Sarah told me that grandmother Natalia would ask May to stop and eat, because she was working so hard, and she was neglecting herself."[104]

As she aged, she suffered a form of dementia, and reportedly even began simply taking things out of retail stores without remembering to pay for them. Ted was embarrassed, and arranged to have her moved to 1008 Chino Street in Santa Barbara, to live with Sarah and Arnold Diaz.[105] Her grandson Sam believes the move to Santa Barbara was also intended to shield her from some of the sickness that his father (and her son) Danny was suffering in the house on Utah Street. When she arrived, she had only two pieces of luggage. Ted had sold or given away everything else, or had it sent to the dump. She had so little, but "with all she had to deal with, she always spoke very positively about the Army and the Lord. Never negative, but so ill. She was a go-getter and she did all she could for the ole Army. That's why she died so darn young and looked so damn old. The Salvation Army took advantage of her ability to get the job done at all cost. I felt bad for her, but she loved the Lord with not one ounce of regret in her heart."[106]

"When Aunt May came to live with us, she was frail. The Salvation Army was her love and her work. She never lost faith even in despair, her love for

Christ was like the Blood & Fire of the old Salvation Army. Many people thought she was crazy. Yeah, with Christ and not drugs or drinking."[107]

There were good memories, though. May could enjoy herself. She was very musical. She had a piano in the living room at Utah Street. She played cornet, guitar and banjo. And, of course, she had "many, many tambourines. We loved playing with those. They made a lot of noise," remembers her nephew Ted. Manuel had his own memories. "She'd play the piano for us. We'd play rock and roll music and she'd say, 'Oh, no. We're going to play hymns.' That's the way she was."

This was the middle to late 50s. She wasn't a big Elvis fan, then? "No. No way. More William Booth. He was the founder. General Kitching, she went to training college with him in Hawaii. He became the commander of the Salvation Army. She'd call him. He was a personal friend. Well, the Army didn't like that – the majors and corporals, they didn't like May going over their heads."

Entertainment was also a feature of her pitch on the street and in visits to bars or other targets. "She would do magic tricks first. Take a cornet with her. And then the next thing, she'd be telling about the Lord. She'd get your attention, capture you and then she'd...She would do a disappearing act with a quarter and she could roll it on her fingers and get your attention with that and then ask you what hand it was in. She would hide it and you'd have to figure out what hand she had it in. She'd laugh at you, "ah ha ha" – it was fun. That's the way she'd get your attention, and then she'd play a little violin or something. It was always a big thing when May came."[108]

When she got preaching, though, she must have been something. Let's allow Manuel to provide a flavor of what it might have been like. "May was a soldier in the Salvation Army and her battle was to enlighten the people around her about the Lord and the wages of Sin – to bring Salvation, so a sinner can repent and prepare to be a Christian. Since May was a simple-type person who took her orders very seriously, she always worked from early morning to late at night and often forgot to eat a decent meal. Her thoughts were to bring people closer to the Lord, because someday you will meet the King of Kings.

"When I was 10 years old I was told no more selling papers on Sunday. The Salvation Army Sunday School was waiting for me at the corner of Chapala and Haley. May told me often that there is no prejudice because, 'If you prick the surface of our skin, we all have red blood no matter what our color is.' I can hear her telling me that right now as I write. When he was inducted into the Baseball Hall of Fame, Ted talked about prejudice and how the game of baseball must open the doors to minorities and allow others to play the great game of baseball, because he had the insight to realize that baseball would some day be played all over the world. Now you see players from poverty-stricken countries in the big leagues. I guess Mom's teachings just might have rubbed off on the Kid from North Park playground.

"May was so directed that others even in the Army were jealous of her. She could easily raise money for the church and had friends in prominent places who would always have time for May Williams. Ted is a real product of his upbringing and even if he did not have an eight to five mom, the Kid from San Diego still got a baptism about the word 'giving' and helping the 'the poor souls and unfortunates!'

Sarah and May, sister musicians with a cause.

"When I asked May if she was embarrassed about singing on the street corner, she said that, 'I am proud to sing praises to the Lord.' As I walked out of her room, I was beginning to realize what this little Christian woman was all about and how she felt so needed.

"When May came to retire and stay at our home, she was just a shadow of herself, but mention the words 'Blood and the Fire' and the Woman of The Year in San Diego would raise her hand up to Jesus and say 'Amen!'"[109]

And she was really in a state of peace with herself and her world. Her nephew Ted provides a wonderful appreciation of May from his own childhood. "In that side bedroom at Utah Street, that bedroom that was Dan and Ted's, that's where they used to put me to take my naps. There was a little twin bed in there. It was a tiny room and it had these kind of paper curtains that came down on the roll, with a cotton ball at the bottom on a string. I never wanted to take a nap, so I lay there just looking at the light. I always noticed that the curtains would blow in the wind and sail out. It was very peaceful and the light would come through – the light was very beautiful in that room, before they built the big apartment house next door.

"I guess I always admired May for her religious beliefs, just that she was so driven by it. She so believed and she was so strong. It was always in her conversation. She wasn't preachy, but she always included the Lord in everything that she said. Her life, and what she wanted out of life, and how people should live. It wasn't, 'You're doing wrong.' It was really just from joy.

"I think she was blessed. She was blissed out with the Lord. I used to lie there sometimes trying to go to sleep, in this dreamlike state, and I imagined this angel coming into the room and touching me, and making me blessed like May was. It was such a beautiful thing. It really was. She was beautiful in this way. It wasn't fire and damnation. It was just love and beauty, and support.

"She'd glow. She radiated. Her eyes sparkled. She was very special."[110]

One son turned out to be a Hall of Fame baseball player, a decorated Marine Corps jet fighter-bomber pilot and a world class sport fisherman – and a leading fundraiser for the fight against cancer in children. The other proved to be a bit of a tough customer and a hard-luck case; he died relatively young, leaving behind a widow and two – it turns out, three – children. We can only speculate how the other two Williams children – be they male or female – might have developed, had they lived.

May died nearly a year and a half after her youngest son, Danny, succumbed to leukemia. Of course, she knew he was seriously ill and undergoing treatment. That awareness may have contributed in part to her own enervation; she may have suffered a nervous breakdown of some sort. Mercifully, though, she may never have known of Danny's death, since she had been relocated to Santa Barbara before his passing. It is the understanding of both sons Sam and Ted that she was never informed of the loss.[111]

THE OTHER VENZORS / MAY'S BROTHERS AND SISTERS

Pedro Venzor   (January 31, 1889 - June 8, 1958)

Pedro [Pete] was the oldest, born in Chihuahua in 1889. He was the cowboy. Pete Venzor and his wife Lupe [Guadalupe Huerta, December 12, 1899-October 20, 1970] had no children. They "married too late," Connie Matthews explained. Pete became foreman at the Tecolote Ranch in Santa Barbara. Owned by the Spaulding family, and also called the Spaulding Ranch, this was quite a large ranch with a great stable. Like his Uncle Rayo Hernandez, who had been a rancher in Mexico, Pete was skilled at the trade. As foreman, he was "the brains of the outfit" and Lupe was the cook, not only for the Spauldings but for the ranch workers as well. At one time or another, at least six of Pete's siblings worked on the ranch. The only two who did not were May and brother Daniel.

Pedro was known as Pedro to close family members, but to most everybody else, he was Pete Venzor. When he was younger, he showed some skill with a game of ball. Sarah talked about Pete's skills at handball. "My oldest brother learned how to play, because here in Santa Barbara we had a lot of Basques. They were all in business. They all had liquor stores. They used to play handball. Not racquetball. Handball. My father used to make the balls for them. They'd start with a little rubber thing inside and he'd wind the twine around it. Then he'd cut the skins and he'd sew them like a baseball, but they were for handball. Not with a racquet, no. Handball."[112]

"The game of handball is a Basque game," Manuel chimed in later. "They take great pride in being the best in the world. The original ball was as hard as a rock and was tough on the hands. My friend was a national champion and he had great respect for the old ball that is no longer used in the game of today. The hand and eye coordination of the Basque is said to be exceptional. They are a very confident people, and their manner and attitude were also of a loner nature. Sound familiar to you?"[113]

Pete apparently had the opportunity to go on the road playing handball. "One priest -- I don't remember his name – came to my mother and asked permission, could he take Pete around the world, to different countries, just as a handball player, just to show his ability and to show how well he could do. He was perfect." Sarah said that Natalia wouldn't give her permission to let the priest take Pete on tour. Pete was too young. "He was a great one and could not be beat," added Manuel. "He ruled the court."[114]

Ted's uncles were avid participants in sports. Three played baseball and one played handball. Young Teddy Williams spent portions of his summer time with cousins and uncles on the Tecolote Ranch. Even when not at the ranch, Ted got in time to play ball with Saul, Paul and Bruno at 1008 Chino Street, and one or more of May's brothers would visit San Diego from time to time.

Pete was an expert shot with a rifle, and was considered to have unusually good vision. He served in World War I. After receiving his training as a soldier, he was sent to France to fight and was scheduled to be advanced to the front when the Armistice was signed and he was returned to Santa Barbara. Brother Daniel was not as fortunate.

Pete's vision served him well on the ranch. It was said that he could post a fence line straight as an arrow without the use of a transit. One senses a bit of a connection to Ted Williams here. Ted had uncommonly good eyesight as well, and he had a very precise sense of distance and alignment – stories abound regarding his ability to estimate distances (and weights) with astonishing accuracy.

For example, there is the story of how Ted, upon returning to baseball after being away for most of two seasons while flying combat missions in Korea, immediately declared that home plate at Fenway Park was not properly situated. The season was more than half over, and not a single other player had complained. They thought Ted was kidding, but he insisted and when measurements were taken, Ted was proven right. Home plate was 1/4 inch out of proper alignment.

Another trait of Pete's that Ted embraced was his insistence on punctuality. Ted Williams was always on time, and he expected others to be on time as well. Pete's sister Sarah, when she worked as a housekeeper at the Tecolote Ranch, recalls that when Pete brought her to town, "you had better be at that certain place for a ride back home. He wouldn't wait, and would simply leave you behind." Manuel Herrera said Pete Venzor "was a kind person and he was stern and meant what he said." If you weren't there on time, you just didn't get your ride back to the ranch. This was not impatience, but just an insistence on the respect implicit in punctuality.

Pete Venzor, sister May, mother Natalia and wife Lupe at 4121 Utah Street.

Manuel respected Pedro Venzor. "Pedro was a patient person and a thinker. He was confident but not a bragging type of person. He knew his talents and could rely on them when needed. He did drink, but he never got out of control and was a quiet man. I liked the guy. He was always kind to me and would invite me to stay at the Tecolote Ranch and enjoy a wonderful homemade meal that his wife made, my Aunt Lupe. Boy, could she cook some great Mexican food! I ate to my heart's content, usually with the work crew near the creek where the picnic tables were set up. If you took time to look up during the evening meal, you could see the deer up the creek in the canyon, drinking water." Of all the various aunts and uncles in the Venzor clan, Manuel felt he was treated best by Pedro and Lupe. "Maybe it was because they had no children," he reflected, "or because they liked my love of the ranch and my wanting to stay with them there."[115]

Manuel continued: "I don't think Ted could beat Pedro in handball, because no one ever did! He was confident but not a bragging type of person. He knew his talents and could rely on them when needed. When my son was born, I took him over to the west side of Santa Barbara to visit Aunt Lupe. She was alone then; Pedro had died of throat cancer. She was very happy to see me and got to hold my son in her arms. She cried and we talked of old times at the ranch. I will never forget that wonderful day!"

The ranch, like Chino Street, was a focal point for the family. Sarah worked as a cleaning lady for Mr. Spaulding. "It seems that the whole Venzor family worked at the Tecolote Ranch. I know that Pete, Lupe, Aunt Sarah, Jenny, Saul, Paul, and Bruno all were employed at the ranch at one time or another. It was Paul who loved the ranch, but Pete was the brains of the outfit. Lupe was the cook and also cooked for the hired help at the ranch, Mom was the cleaning lady for Mr. Spaulding, he had a big home on the hill to the right of the ranch as you face the entrance."[116]

Sarah had already confirmed this. "We all worked out there at Tecolote Ranch. That was run by Mr. Spaulding. He was married to a very rich girl. She had more money than he did. They had one daughter, Deborah. They had a beautiful ranch. My oldest brother Pete had a very good eye. He'd be the one to take care of the Mexican help that used to go and work there, because he had a large avocado [grove] up against the hill. He was right close against the ocean, too. Mr. Spaulding had oil wells there along the coast, right across the street...the freeway went right through his property. That's where the Japs attacked Tecolote Ranch, in Goleta."[117]

Perhaps May Venzor learned how to be comfortable around governors and other political figures, because of some familiarity with them at the ranch.

"There were some special barbecues at the Tecolote Ranch, where Ted spent time running around. [There was] lots of room to run and chase cattle, or pick walnuts like I did. Mr. Spaulding hosted the Commanders' Barbecue for the California Highway Patrol and the Governor. Chill Wills, Will Rogers, Bud McSpadden, Dick Carr, Monty Montana and other notables from Hollywood came, and cowboys and screen and political people from the state capitol. Uncle Pete ran the program and did something that people do not do any more -- he cooked a cow, underground. It's not done now, because it's too much work. Pete knew how and I was told that's the best way to cook beef; the meat falls right off the bone. Lupe Venzor could make the best tamales and menudo, along with a mole poblano that made me come to the ranch just to enjoy her homemade dishes. Her job was to cook for the ranch hands, but I would stand by her when she began serving and I always got invited for her special meal. My mouth still remembers that wonderful food."[118]

Pedro Venzor used to smoke Bull Durham tobacco and apparently it got him in the end. He died of cancer of the throat at the Sawtell Veterans Hospital in West Los Angeles. He is buried at the Santa Barbara Cemetery, as is his father.

Pete had some talent at music, as well.

Mary Venzor Cordero (April 18, 1893 - October 7, 1943)

The oldest girl in the family was born Maria Venzor. Ted's Aunt Mary came to a tragic end, but not before bearing a "baker's dozen" – thirteen children – one of whom (Anita) was Manuel Herrera's mother. She married Albert Cordero, who worked as a trucker. Teresa Cordero Contreras was the youngest of the brood and she recalls, "Albert, my father, he had a trucking outfit. Local. Through Santa Barbara County and Los Angeles. He had seven trucks. He struggled through the Depression; then the war came and it took away three of my brothers, took them away from the trucking business. So we had to take over -- the girls. We did all we could, but my dad lost a lot during that time."[119]

It was the effort to save the firm that may have contributed to the murder/suicide which took Mary Venzor's life and robbed Manuel Herrera of his mother as well. "We were working in the fruit up north," Teresa Contreras continues. "Up north in Fairfield, picking plums, peaches, everything we could – because we had to help my dad, for the trucks that he had. He had to pay the State Board of Equalization for everything, and he had to keep the house up. My brothers had gone off to war. There was no one else, so us girls had to help. My sister Annie [Anita] had to move down from Stockton to Fairfield to work a little bit. She could make you laugh. She had a sense of humor. She was silly. She made us all laugh.

"My dad stayed back in Santa Barbara, and we went up north to work with the fruit. He used to haul away anything that was sacked or baled. He'd haul grains, alfalfa, hay, barley, beans. Ted knew my dad. I think he was kind of close to my dad, and my mom -- more than he was to my Aunt Jean or Uncle Paul."

In a later interview, Ted's cousin Teresa added, "My dad was a cowboy, you know. His father was a rancher. He was born in Las Cruces, California, right on the ranch. He used to haul for different ranches out there. He did that until he got married. I know he used to deliver milk, too. That's how he met my mom. Delivering milk and cheese. She was living in Santa Barbara; they were on Montecito Street at that time."[120] Albert then got into the trucking business full-time.

Annie Cordero – Teresa's sister – had married Salvador Herrera, who may have misunderstood his wife's departure to help save the family firm. Anita and Sal Herrera had six children: Mary [Redding], Salvador [Sal, Jr.],

"The picture of Pete with his guitar, Saul, Paul and Natalia was taken next door at 1006 Chino Street at Bruno's place in the back yard. The palm tree is to the right of the group and the picnic tables were under the slat swing that is directly behind them. I helped Bruno build the gazebo. This was about 1954 in Santa Barbara, CA. Uncle Pete gave his guitar to Arnold just before he passed away. Every time I drove by the place I remembered Uncle Pete. Pete often brought his guitar to play music with Arnold R. Diaz. They played my favorite, "Zacatecas." It is the National Anthem of Mexico. I first heard it played by Uncle Pete at the Tecolote ranch at the age of maybe 4 or 5. I liked Uncle Pete to play the song for me and in later years that old song brought back some fond memories of the ranch and Uncle Pete and Aunt Lupe and her cooking. I was next to Mom when she took this picture."
– Manuel Herrera

Kathleen [Osowski], Paul, and twins Manuel and Natalie. There was a seventh child, Carmen, but she passed away as a baby. These were difficult times and Salvador Herrera was out of work. Mary Redding says, "My dad spoke very little English, and we did not speak Spanish. On both sides, Spanish was spoken by the adults but not by the children."[121]

The work with fruit evokes the image of migrant workers and perhaps, within the state of California, that is what they were at this particular point in time. "We didn't pick apricots, but we cut them in half. Put them on trays. We picked peaches. We cut peaches also. We picked pears. We picked plums. We picked grapes." Apparently, Anita and her mother Mary went back to Anita's home together. "She told my mom, 'We've got to get some more clothes for the kids.' Well, Mr. Herrera took it wrong, I guess. I don't know what it was. We didn't get word until the next morning what had happened."[122] On a Sunday in October 1943, at 505 South Wilson Way in

Stockton, Sal Herrera shot his wife, his mother-in-law, and then took his own life.

"He used an old-fashioned gun from Mexico," Teresa reports. "He used to drink a lot. Wine. I guess it was just depression, because he wasn't working. Only God knows why. She was everybody's favorite [Anita]. It was always so nice to have her around. When she died, I was 13. As soon as my mom passed on, my dad brought us home. And there was no more fruit."[123]

The Corderos were native Californians, Teresa explained, and they trace the lineage back to 1765, when "the first forefather arrived here in 1765 with Father Serra as one of the leatherjackets with the Patrol Army. My forefather was a corporal. They came from Spain. They arrived in Mexico City. He married in Baja to a Mexican woman, and they came up here to California. His son married an Indian here, the princess of the Chumash Indian tribe. He was here when they were building the missions. That was in the 1780s or 1790s." So there's even a bit of royalty in the greater Ted Williams family!

Albert Cordero couldn't handle all of the young Herreras as well as his own children, so they were distributed out among other relatives. Albert took in Mary Herrera. Kathleen and Paul went to live with John Cordero. Sal, Jr. was taken in by Rayo Hernandez. Manuel and Natalie went to live with Natalia Venzor, and when she died, they lived with Sarah and Arnold Diaz.

Most of the children suffered not only the initial trauma but other difficulties as well, within the homes they were placed. Mary was faced with a grandfather prepared to abuse her, and in the seventh grade – as soon as she could -- she took employment as a mother's helper with another family. When she turned 18, that job ran out and she went to live with her aunt Jeanne Venzor Winet.

The Herrera family was fully fractured. The children weren't in close touch with each other at all. Manuel and his twin sister Natalie went to the center of the Venzor family, though, and spent over 10 years with Natalia Venzor at 1008 Chino Street before she passed away, then continued living at

Mary and May Venzor, Santa Barbara.

Chino Street with Sarah and Arnold. This location positioned Manuel well to soak up some of the family lore.

Manuel tells the tale of when he later met his brother Paul after a long separation. "I don't think you know how important a baseball field was in my young life," Manuel wrote me. "The game for me was always fun and I was interested in finding out how good I could play the game of baseball. Since Ted Williams was a great player and my oldest brother [Sal Herrera] played professional baseball for over eight years, I felt I had some talent for the game. Little did I know that baseball had more to offer than the game.

"In the Santa Barbara city recreational program, we had a midget league during the 50s which consisted of kids in the 9- to 12-year-old age bracket. Well, I was selected to play for the Kiwanis Club and my first game was to be at Santa Barbara Junior High School. We were playing the Lions team and I was looking forward to the game. Gosh, I was only 9 years old and the coach put me out in right field where I wouldn't make a mistake by dropping a fly ball or whatever might go wrong!

"I don't think I hit the ball at all while at bat, but while sitting on the bench waiting for my turn at bat, a voice came to my ears. Someone called my name out. Sure enough, it was my uncle, John Cordero. I had seen him only maybe two or three times but I recognized him quickly. He told me, 'Your brother Paul is the second baseman on the other team; he is your older brother.' I was shocked to say the least. I had heard that I had a brother, but as a kid who knows when you will ever met the person or it might not be true, who knows?

"An idea flashed in my mind. I was going to stop the second baseman and tell him he was my brother. I did just that and I said, 'Hey, Paul I'm your brother Manuel.' He just looked at me and laughed as he said, 'Way to go, brother' as he ran into the dugout.

"Yeah, it was a pretty emotional game and meeting my brother was bigger than the game of baseball, but the American pastime brought us together for the first time in our young lives. What a special event!"[124]

Ted Williams knew Annie Cordero. They liked each other and were good friends as cousins. "She could really run," recalls Manuel. "Ted liked her, because she could hit a baseball." She was a bit of a tomboy. With a dad for a trucker, the girls as well as the boys learned how to drive. Ted taught her how to hit a baseball and the two of them sometimes rode around Santa Barbara together in a car, even driving up on the sidewalk for fun. "Ted loved that!" Teresa was a lot younger, born in 1929. She remembers Ted visiting the small house her family had at 1716 Chino Street. "He had to stoop under the eaves to get in. He lifted me up and said, 'Now you can touch the ceiling!' I remember that."[125]

In general, though, Manuel says that the Venzors and Corderos were not that close. "My grandfather [Albert] was a very hard working man. He would unload a freight car of, say, potatoes, and load it onto one of his trucks and haul it up north, usually to Atascadero or Paso Robles. I remember him bringing kindling for the old wooden stove we used at the house at 1008 Chino Street. He would unload the kindling and afterwards come in and have a morning cup of

Sal Herrera and Annie C. Herrera with children Mary, Salvador Jr., and Kathleen, summer, 1941.

101

Poster on storefront advertising conference in Parral.
Photograph by Ted Williams.

L to R: Raul Herrera Morales (historian of El Valle de Allende), Bill Nowlin, Señor Gildardo Valles, Ted Williams, Doctor Jesus Gamez.

At the conference in Parral, L to R: Bill Nowlin, translator Lorena Chavez, Ted Williams.

At the Presidencia Municipal de Parral. L to R: Sr. Rigo Rivas,
Ricardo Urquidi, Jose Hicks, Ted Williams, Bill Nowlin.

Plaza Principal, Valle de Allende.
Photograph by Bill Nowlin.

In Valle de Allende.
Photograph by Ted Williams.

Street scene, Valle de Allende.
Photograph by Bill Nowlin.

coffee. He would always show grateful respect to his mother-in-law Natalia. I liked his manners and sincere ways." Manuel blames the failure of the trucking business on Albert's "no-account sons [who] ran it into the ground before their father died of a heart attack." Manuel's middle name is Albert, after his grandfather. Manuel's twin sister Natalie was named after Natalia Hernandez Venzor, and her middle name is Jean, for Aunt Jeanne Venzor.

Losing both Mary and Annie was a big loss, and to have lost them in such a shocking way was devastating to the family. Pete was "kind" but Mary had a really big heart, like her sisters May and Sarah. "Mary and May were the true givers in the old family," Manuel wrote me. "Mary my grandmother was very much like Natalia. She would go all over town helping friends and neighbors. My Uncle Arnold said, 'Mary would give you her soul.' She loved horses and had a stallion on the ranch; one time it almost killed her, trampling her, but she came out of it. Though Natalia and her oldest daughters May and Mary had such big hearts, and Sarah as well – though to a lesser degree – "the rest of the family stood alone and never were close. Time and events took a large toll on the Venzor family."[126]

While Ted was still living, Manuel wrote me, "May spent 50 years in the Salvation Army and I really think Teddy resents the fact that the ole Army kept her from developing a family home and normal life style. She was a simple person and was so darn loyal to her cause! Mary, my grandmother, was cut from the same mold and she would drive around Santa Barbara helping the needy and poor families, while her kids tore up the house! They called her a 'santa' or in English a saint. Natalia was just like Mary, then May, but the rest were not even close to the older girls."[127]

Mary's daughter Teresa remembers her mother being active, "even with the hoboes. We lived about six blocks from the train tracks. They would come around and knock on our back door, and my mother would give them coffee and things that they could take. She would collect things and give them. She was a very loving person, just a thoughtful person."[128]

"The family members were loners and very cold hearted. They often never conversed with each other or didn't take the time to. Mary and May were the true givers in the old family, then Sarah but not to the liking of her older sisters. The rest of the family stood alone and never were close, time and events took a large toll on the manners of the Venzor family. Most of the siblings are of the same nature; they don't know how to show one bit of love or family relationship. I really don't know why, but that has been the trend for many years. They stood alone!

"My father murdered my mother Annie and he destroyed my grandmother. He did commit suicide and left six kids to face unhappy homes and alcoholic families. There is something about not feeling a part of a family and that was always present in my heart and soul."[129]

Being farmed out to families produced some uneven results and some unhappy results. Mary Herrera spent those seven years as a mother's helper. "I finished school while I worked for Commander George & Mrs. Collins, who lived in Montecito and was a mother's helper for her and her three children – Ann, Winslow, Gina. There was never any love shown to me, I knew my place and stayed there. I was more or less the housekeeper and cleanup crew. Never ever remember any one in the family giving me a hug or any affection."[130]

Manuel sometimes wished he'd been raised in an orphanage, instead of where he was taken in. He wrote me, "You should have been there to live the experiences that my sister and I had to put up with! I feel robbed of trust and the family image I wanted. The abusive people who wanted me to be their son. When the responsibilities came, you couldn't find one family member to support your effort. I had plenty of criticism and negative input from Sarah alone, not to bring up Arnold and the drinking and abuse he offered his wife. Arnold did his own thing at the expense of the family and yet when he was home, he wanted everything right and proper. I liked Pop as a friend, but he was not a father figure and his lifestyle came first.

"I really think that being in an orphanage might have been a more positive way of life to me. Ted is easily fooled, and the fact that he didn't even call or write his mother hurts me for a person who did more for humanity than he could ever offer!"[131]

There was another family member, one of Ted's cousins, who by all accounts had a real shot at becoming a major league ballplayer.

Sal Herrera, Jr. connects a couple of worlds. He was, by all accounts, an exceptionally talented baseball player who might have made it to the majors if he hadn't been so volatile. He also has a bit of the horseman in him. Retired from more than 40 years work as a glazier, working on high rise buildings, he and his wife Edna live in Elko, Nevada. Sal enjoys raising two horses, a prize-winning stallion and a filly.

His brother Manuel told me that Sal was a true baseball prospect. Taken in by Rayo Hernandez, Sal played eight years for the Braves organization and one year with the Dodgers. He nearly made it to the major leagues – a great athlete, but his own worst enemy. Sal also lived for a year or two with Bruno Venzor's family. Bruno's son, Danny, about five years older than Sal, recalls, "We used to pitch to each other as hard as we could. Sal was really a hell of a ballplayer. I think it was the same scout who signed Eddie Mathews who signed Sal. But Sal had a hell of a temper. There's not too many managers in the minor leagues that would take him on. This guy was big and strong, had a killer arm and could hit. He has all the tools. He played outfield – center field – but the guy just had a temper that he couldn't control. That's probably the main reason why he didn't even get a chance. He got kicked out of baseball."[132]

Sal played center field at Santa Barbara High School and was an All-CIF first team player, coming in second for player of the year to Marty Keough, who played first base for the Boston Red Sox and the Cincinnati Reds. Sal was the MVP of the Pomona tournament - the same tournament in which Ted Williams had played more than fifteen years earlier. He was reportedly signed as a non-roster "bonus baby" by the Braves, right out of high school, though

I have been unable to confirm this with old Milwaukee Braves researchers. Still, the specificity of the detail provided me by Manuel, by Danny Venzor and by others is hard to deny. Sal was good friends with Eddie Mathews and roomed for a while with Warren Spahn, traveling with the big league club although he never appeared in a game.

"Sal should have been a Hall of Famer – [I don't say that] because he was my brother, but because he had the tools. But you can't scream at the fans and run after them with a bat in the stands. He had all the tools but, his attitude cost him the majors."[133]

Daniel Venzor   (May 30, 1895 - November 11, 1918)

The first Venzor of his generation to die was Daniel. He never had a chance to realize himself in life, since he died in combat during the First World War. Sadly, his death came after the war was over. Serving in France, he dodged one bullet right near the end of the war, and lived to write home about it. That was his last letter home.

Daniel Venzor is listed as having been killed on November 11, 1918 – the very date the Armistice was signed. The reality, though, was that he was killed sometime in the four or five days after the war was officially over.[134] After signing the peace accords, communication was late in reaching the front lines due to the more limited methods of communication available at the time, and when word finally did arrive, many German troops did not believe it and so continued on fighting. When Daniel was killed, Ted Williams was about 10 or 11 weeks old.

An allotment provided by the United States government and paid out over several years was sufficient to finance the 1920 purchase of the house and property at 1008 Chino Street for Daniel's mother and father, and that home became the center of the family, despite Pablo Venzor's death that same year.

That house at 1008 Chino Street remained that center, even after Natalia Venzor passed on. Sarah and Arnold lived there, with Manuel and Natalie Herrera. Bruno Venzor and his wife Marian lived at 1006 Chino Street while

Paul and Tillie Venzor were at 1002 Chino. "We were one big happy family there in three homes," said Paul's son Frank.[135]

Natalia chose not to have Daniel's body returned home to America, because she thought that might further disturb his remains, so he is buried in France, in Flanders Field. A dozen or so years after the war, Natalia was offered a trip to France to visit the gravesite, and she accepted. May Williams accompanied her mother as far as El Paso, Connie Matthews remembers. Natalia joined with other Gold Star mothers – mothers who had lost a child in the war – and took a train to New York and then a ship to England. She made her way to France and was able to visit Daniel's grave at the American military cemetery. A photographer noticed her praying at his grave, and he captured the image. It became a fairly well-known photograph and has reportedly been exhibited at the National Gallery of Art in Washington and elsewhere.

Manuel says, "When my precious Natalia returned from Europe, she viewed the Statue of Liberty and cried, for she was home again on hallowed ground. She well knew the meaning of freedom and the price her son paid for that gift. She had left Mexico because of the revolution and the killings that were occurring at that time and America was her salvation from war."[136] Ironically, 30 years later, war took her son.

Ironically as well, Manuel and Natalie Herrera -- the twins -- were both born on November 11. It was never a purely enjoyable day for them. On their sixth birthday, Manuel remembers, "My sister and I usually had a cake for our birthday. Mine was chocolate and my sister's was always a white cake. I can't even remember getting a gift, but that is not important. I was really looking forward to the big day and the cake. That evening after supper we gathered around the table and the 'Happy Birthday' song was sung to me and my sister. The candles were blown out and of course on went the lights. I looked at my great-grandmother and tears were streaming down from her eyes and I knew the loss of her son Daniel was in her heart. My birthday didn't matter any longer. I just wanted to be near my precious Natalia and comfort her as she so often did me, so I went to her and put my arms around her and hugged her. I knew nothing had to be said. She needed me more than I needed the cake. She gave me a home and most of all some love and I had the chance to give it back. It was never the same after I lost my Natalia."[137]

Daniel Venzor, sister May (left) and mother Natalia with a grandchild.

"Mom [Sarah] was so hurt and in pain about her brother. She knew he almost made it through the war, but fate dealt a blow that scarred the family forever. From what I know about Daniel, he was more like Pete Venzor in manner and ways. I was told that Daniel was also a very honest person and kinda long and lean in structure. Daniel was so close to making it home, Mom always had that same fear about me being in the Vietnam War with my last days. Yes, she was a worry-wart, but I can understand why, with the devastating lost of her brother in France. It was the tough experiences in life that brought those traits to be a worrisome way in her heart and of course they never did go away!"[138]

Pete Venzor saw duty in France as well. Trained in the United States, he shipped out to France and was due to be sent to the front. Spared by the signing of the Armistice, he was demobilized and returned home to Santa Barbara and the ranch.

Daniel had escaped one close call. He wrote in a letter to his mother that he was almost hit in the head by a bullet. That time, he was spared. The second time Death came calling, he succumbed, killed in action right at the very conclusion of the first World War – tragically, as explained above, some days after peace was officially declared.

Of course, Ted's brother Danny was named after Daniel Venzor. So was Bruno's son Danny. There was also a Danny Cordero as well, Ted's cousin, a son of Mary Venzor and Albert Cordero. Daniel Cordero unfortunately died early, too, falling out of a truck his father was driving, as did Danny Williams, dying at age 39 from leukemia.

Natalia Venzor was honored ever afterward in Santa Barbara as a Gold Star mother. Ruth Gonzales recalls that "during the Spanish fiestas, she would ride with another lady in little horse-drawn carriages with the Mayor of Santa Barbara. The other lady died and then it was just her."[139]

Saul C. Venzor (November 2, 1903 - August 15, 1963)

"The old guy had street smarts and was always on me to repeat my ABC's and this was to be done while my hands were at my side and I stood at attention and I finished with a "YES SIR!" Then it was checkers or Chinese checkers, take your choice – but a 12-inch ruler was at his side if you made a mistake, and little me was often struck on the hand. The old guy never let up on me, and I was often asked, "Do you want the persuader?" and I replied a loud, "No!" I wanted to make sure Uncle Saul heard me!"[140]

"Saul could just look at you and put the fear of God in you," remembers Manuel, not that fondly. "He often made me close the back door 10 times because I slammed it so hard. I was so afraid of the man that I did what he demanded right on the spot. He was not a kind person by any means and he always threatened us kids with the 'persuader.' Hell, I had no idea what a damn persuader was but it must not have been a good thing! He always vowed to use the persuader on us, but we never saw it."[141]

Saul Venzor made a strong impression on everyone around him. He certainly left a strong impression on Manuel Herrera, and so did his "persuader." It's not hard to see how Saul had an important influence on Ted Williams and helped forge some of the drive and determination that characterized Ted's approach to baseball.

He was a longshoreman, and worked with the famous Gang 1 crew that worked in Port Hueneme or in San Pedro, the L. A. port of entry. "The gang he worked for was noted for getting the job well done. They loaded the holds of many a freighter headed to foreign ports during the Second World War and the Korean conflict. Gang 1 was respected and singled out for their work."[142]

Saul was active locally, and managed one of the area baseball teams, the Santa Barbara Merchants. He was the first real baseball player in the Venzor family. Saul Venzor's obituary says that he "is credited with giving famed ballplayer Ted Williams his first baseball lessons" and adds that "Williams, his nephew, was quoted by friends here that Mr. Venzor was his first instructor."[143]

Daniel Venzor.

Ted's Aunt Sarah recalled times Ted came to visit in Santa Barbara. "Ted played with my brother Saul. We made them play out in the field. We had a big garden and we have a long driveway. They'd get out there on the driveway and throw the ball to each other. That's how Ted learned a lot, too, from my brother, about throwing. It's odd how he throws right

Natalia Venzor at Daniel's grave, France.

and hits left. When Ted would come, the first thing they would do is get out there in that field and pitch to each other, throw the ball to each other, and bat to each other. My mother was left-handed, too, and boy, she didn't miss us when she threw rocks at us, trying to get our attention, you know."[144] Sarah's nephew Danny Venzor remembers Natalia's arm, too. "She just spoke Spanish, and she's the one who took care of all the grandkids, because – you know, being poor, all the parents worked. We're all playing ball in the driveway and we had to go up there and get the ball in her garden. There's all these boxes of oranges and lemons. She'd yell at us in Spanish, and we'd run. She threw left-handed. She could hit you running, and hit you in the back. She'd wing it from the porch. We'd be taking off and she could wing a lemon or an orange from the porch and she could nail you. And she was old. She could whip a lemon up there and hit you with it."[145]

Uncle Saul was tough on Ted, and Ted may have learned a few other traits from Saul as a result. Manuel reports stories he learned growing up in the family, "The old guy really had the tools and Teddy would literally beg Saul to teach him how to pitch a baseball. Ted was eager and Saul knew the kid wanted to play baseball more than anything in the world. Saul told Teddy, "Not yet, you're not ready to pitch. I will tell you when I will teach you how to pitch a ball."

One time when Ted was visiting, Saul's wife Henrietta told Manny the story at Saul's daughter's house – Dee Allen's house. She said, "Saul wouldn't give in to Ted and made him wait and plead to learn how to pitch." Manny says he looked at Ted and Ted had a big grin on his face, animated by the memories.[146]

Saul was stubborn and aggressive and talented. Manny says, "No one could beat the guy, and he hated to lose. Saul gave Ted more than just pitching lessons. He used a no-lose attitude to build Ted's confidence and [demonstrate] how to think and win. Not just get the ball over the plate, but to think with your head and always be aggressive." Ted's determination to show his Uncle Saul what he could do has to have played into the single-minded drive which made Ted such a good ballplayer. "Ted had seen him pitch in different games. He would plead, 'Uncle Saul, can I pitch now?' Saul says, 'Aw, you're not ready, kid. Come on back. Come by tomorrow. Come back in another week. Maybe you're not hungry enough.' 'Oh, please, Uncle Saul! I want to be a pitcher. I want to learn how to throw a pitch. I want to learn how to pitch.' He'd tell Ted, 'Oh, maybe another day. Not today.' 'Oh, come on, Uncle Saul! Please!' He'd beg him all day. Ted would throw his glove down and walk out of the room."[147]

Frank Venzor, one of Ted's cousins, confirms Saul's role in molding a young Ted Williams, determined to prove he could be good. "Saul was the one who started this baseball stuff. He was one of the oldest brothers. He was the one who got Ted into baseball. Even before he picked up a ball, before he knew what a glove was. We had a slanted driveway on Chino Street. It looked like a pitcher's mound. Everybody was a pitcher, particularly Saul. They used to put Ted up there. 'Get up there. See if you can hit this,' they would yell at him. They weren't nice to him. They were not nice to him. Ever. They used to tease him. He'd be out there bawling and crying. I get this information from my Aunt Sarah. She said, 'Boy, those guys used to get up there and tease Ted. They'd get him out there on the driveway and he'd be crying. 'Get closer! Get up there! See if you can hit this!' My uncle could throw! He could throw 19 different pitches. This is where Ted began to recognize them. My aunt used to stick her head out the window and say, 'Saul! Leave the kid alone!'"[148]

Teasing or taunting a younger cousin could be discouraging or, if you share a family trait of toughness, independence and stubborn resolve, it can hone a commitment to succeed. Ted's own mother demonstrated single-minded and unswerving dedication in her calling as a Salvationist. It's not surprising that her eldest son picked up many of the same traits and put his own twist on it. "He was determined to be the best baseball player," observed Rosalie Larson, the daughter of May's brother Paul, "and she was determined to be the best captain in the Salvation Army."[149]

Saul Venzor was apparently quite a legend in Santa Barbara. "Ted reminds me a lot of Saul," Manuel Herrera wrote. "Ted is very independent and knows what he liked best – hitting a baseball. Saul was a great pitcher and was very respected as a baseball player here in Santa Barbara. Everyone knew he could pitch and he finally got a chance to show his stuff against the barnstorming major leaguers. He pitched a great game and struck out ole Babe Ruth and a bunch the other so-called heroes of the diamond! The game was played in Santa Barbara about 1935 and I know a few people who remember the game. They were more impressed with Saul Venzor than the major league all-stars.[150]

Frank Venzor recounts another story he heard. "Uncle Saul pitched a 19-inning, 1-0 ball game in the minors against the Los Angeles, the Metro...the railroad company. My dad told me he wouldn't quit. He wouldn't give up. He just pitched the 19 innings all by himself, and they won 1-0. They used to play at Cabrillo Field. They were called the Goleta Merchants. Ted used to send them equipment and balls and gloves."[151]

John Zant's article in the *Santa Barbara News-Press* stated that Saul "was a pitcher who could really bring the heat. He dominated the semipro games in Santa Barbara. 'He had a great arm,' said Tim Badillo, 91, who knew all the ballplayers in town. 'I brought Satchel Paige up here to throw in some games. Saul didn't quite have that good an arm, but he could throw the ball.' Saul has been credited with stoking Williams' interest in baseball when his nephew visited Santa Barbara. Apparently, Saul had some of Satchel Paige's gamesmanship."[152]

One of the games Ted saw Saul pitch is recounted in a story Saul's son-in-law David Allen tells. David is married to Saul's daughter Dee, who was for years an active local softball player herself. David relates a story Ted told at a family reunion: "He said that Saul was pitching at a semipro game, and he

UPBMI Baseball Team, Santa Barbara. Left to right, standing: Isaias Castillo, Sam Robinero, Poncho Osuna, Saul Venzor, Gene Lillard, Marion Hill. Seated: Fred Cuevas, Manuel Mendoza, Julius Sesma, Duke Dally, Albert Castillo, Esque Escobar, Eddie Cuevas, Henry Becerra, Ginger Romero.

walked the bases loaded with nobody out. Then he asked the umpire for a time-out, and he went over to the opposing bench. He said, 'I'm betting that you guys don't score. Who wants to take me up on it?' He collected all these bets, and he went out and struck out the next batter. Then, he either struck out two more or got a double play, Ted didn't remember. But he won the bet."[153] Dee confirmed that Ted was at that game, and watched it first-hand. It had to have made a real impression on young Teddy Williams.[154]

According to his obituary in the *News-Press*, Zant notes, "Saul Venzor turned down an offer to play in the Coast League with Lefty O'Doul."[155]

Could Saul have made it in pro ball? Maybe. But love got in the way. Saul was enamored of Henrietta Osuna and wanted to marry, but when he was offered a deal, there were a couple of other beaus seeking her favors. Saul was afraid to leave, Henrietta told Manuel Herrera. She also confirmed Saul's role in helping mold Ted. "She and Saul often trekked down to San Diego to visit May and the boys. She and I conversed about the trips to San Diego and how Teddy would beg Saul to teach him how to pitch a baseball. Saul would tell Ted, 'Not yet, kid. You're not ready to pitch. Just wait, your time will come' and his Uncle Saul made him wait and wait. He taught Ted the basic pitches - fastball, curve and slider. Saul and Ted got along very well; since everything was all baseball, they had a lot in common."

The marriage ended in divorce, though. "It was the bottle or the family. Saul wanted the family, but he couldn't stop drinking and he lost everything and his family as well. As a young man Saul was very strict and he only told you one time if you made a mistake! When I knew him for almost 11 years he was just a shadow of himself and the wine took its toll on him. He was a cold person when I knew him and made my life very unhappy, too."[156]

It's tragic that the marriage did not work out. Frank Venzor called Henrietta "the kindest, gentlest, most noble person that walked the face of the earth. Her family owned a tortilla shop or tamale shop and one of them was located in Texas. Macaroni, corn tortillas, and they used to feed people if they were hungry, that didn't have anything. They ended up putting up a shop in Santa

Barbara on the east side of town."[157] When the breakup occurred, Saul moved into 1008 Chino Street and there he stayed for about 10 years. Finally, it became unbearable and he had to be asked to move out.

"I saw Uncle Saul sitting on a bus bench many times. Heck, I used to be the runner for his dollar. It was like this: the phone would ring and it was Saul. He wanted a buck to win some money. One dollar; that was all he needed to make some big bucks. He was hustling a game of snooker at the Golden Lion pool hall on State Street, playing his favorite game. Saul was the best player around at one time, relentless in his game. I heard if you got the guy mad, when he didn't get his money, the next thing you knew – bam! – he would drop you and knock you down. The word was Uncle Saul was fast, lighting fast with his mitts and not to be messed with – and no one could beat him at snooker. He was injured on the job and was disabled, and he was so good no one would play him, so he traveled all over the coast to hustle a buck. He often left town and traveled from San Diego to Portland. He won big time, but the wine bottle never left."[158]

One of the reasons he traveled out of town is because the other players around San Diego caught on. Saul was just too good. Bruno often tagged along. About 5'8" or 5'9", he didn't look much like Saul, who was long and lean and about 6'3". Dee told me, "Bruno was my father's shill. My dad got to be so good that nobody in Santa Barbara would play with him. So Bruno and him would go like to Santa Maria or some of these other outlying places. My dad always made sure he lost one or two before he cleaned up."[159]

"Saul could have done anything he wanted," Manuel wrote, "but the wine took him over. He was lightning fast with his hands and could drop a guy over an argument as quick as a cat. He was very agile and loved to play thinking games. Snooker was his game and he won the city tournaments every time he entered the event. He was smart and quick to learn and he had a reputation. But Saul got old and his drinking got worse, till he hated life and made everyone miserable. He wore black frisco jeans and a white longshoreman's cap with a white or blue shirt all the time. When he hurt his leg as a longshoreman, it was over for him.

"Saul was built lean like Ted and he was about 6' 3" but still lean as he grew older. He was very positive about what he knew and was always thinking. All the cops knew him and they would often stop and bid him a hello. I was the one who took the smokes and hard candy when he was in the county jail. I hated that job, but my Mom made me do it. I still have nightmares when I dream about the place. It scared me to walk on the stone cold floor and no light and very dark to boot! I was only 5 or 6 years old but I have woken up

Dee Allen, Saul's daughter, playing baseball in Santa Barbara.

many a time in a cold sweat over that experience. I always gave the brown bag to the guard, usually a big guy with a dark uniform and a cold looking appearance!"

Saul had a strong hand in forming Ted as a determined ballplayer. "I really do think Saul had a lot to do with building Ted's attitude toward the game of baseball," Manuel wrote. "I could see he was quick minded, a thinker and not happy just to do things, anything. It had to be done right and no mistakes. He played life like that to the hilt. He had an obsession to do it right and understand what you were doing, you know, why and it had to be right. I always had to say my ABC's in front of him and boy I could leave only after I did it right. I think Saul was trying to prove his worth, but the drinking caused conflicts and his age and bad leg caught up to him. I know near the end he tried to stop drinking, and he did for maybe nine months. It was just too late for him. He once told me Ted was a hell of a baseball player and he started thinking and just smiled at me, as he said, 'Ted, he was just a kid.' And he looked right in my eyes. I could see he was proud of the help [he gave and the] association he had with his nephew. He would never get soft. He wasn't one to look for a pat on the back. That wasn't Saul's style. He lived to win and never looked back.

"One evening I entered a restaurant and Charles Venzor [Saul's son] was at the counter eating. We acknowledged each other and got to talking and Uncle Saul came up. I asked Charles, 'Did you really know your father?' He looked at me and said, 'No, you lived with him and probably knew him better than I did.' I then realized that I did know old Saul pretty darn well. He was a loner and hard to deal with, you didn't make mistakes – and no losing, either! That was not his manner and I am sure it rubbed off on Ted. Hell, they played baseball all the time and that is all they talked about. They did have a lot in common and built a great relationship together."[160]

The last time Ted and Saul met was at May Williams' funeral in 1961. Ted had come to town and rented the entire top floor at the Santa Barbara Inn, so he wouldn't be bothered. Only the aunts and uncles were permitted to attend the funeral itself. The rest of the family waited at 1008 Chino Street. There was, of course, a reason for this: there was "a ton of reporters" at the entrance to the funeral home, and one of them was so bold as to ask his Aunt Sarah, "Did Ted cry at the wake?"[161]

Danny Venzor told John Zant, "He was staying at the Santa Barbara Inn under a fictitious name. I remember he got mad when a stranger showed up on the second floor. He rented every room on the floor so nobody would bother him. When we got there, he was standing in his undershirt at this big bay window overlooking East Beach. He could see his reflection in the window. He was swinging an imaginary bat, just to relax."[162]

Ted made his way from the hotel to Chino Street, where most of the relatives awaited him. "A white Ford pulled down the driveway and a big good-looking guy made his way out," Manuel Herrera remembers clearly. "I walked outside to greet the Slugger. He was dressed for travel and the family came out of the old house and visited him. Bruno and Marian Venzor were there, along with Mom and Pop. Natalie and I were introduced to him by Mom. Everything was baseball to him, even his vocabulary, too. He called Saul 'Old-Timer' and wanted to know how he was doing. Saul acknowledged his welcome and smiled. He told Ted, 'You did pretty good for yourself, kid, in the big leagues.' Ted, with a twinkle in his eyes, said, 'Yeah, old-timer, I guess I did all right, Saul, thanks.' Uncle Saul was like the old professor with his prime student and you could see the gleam on his face when he said, 'I see that you learned how to hit the curve ball, and you did pretty good, huh?' Now Ted was looking right at Saul as if to say, thanks for all you did for me. Teddy had a big grin on his face, focused right at Saul.

"It was like the old teacher and the student measuring his success of the seasons of the past. I was standing between Saul and Ted. I can't tell you the emotion that was in each man's eyes and the look they showed that day. I could feel it in the air and on their faces. It was a moment to behold. I lived with Saul for 11 or 12 years and knew him like the back of my hand. There was a time to stay away from him and a time to do as he said. He was a tough old guy but that one day he was human, after all that was said and done. He sure wasted a good life, sorry to say."[163]

Saul asked Ted a few questions, and this is the one question I remember. He said, "Ted, a ball can only go four different ways – in, out, up or down. What is a palm ball, a sinker and a screw ball?" Ted was very happy with the question and said, "Saul, that is a great question. They are only curve balls thrown a bit differently, but the announcers make something more of it. Hell, they can't tell what the damn pitch is from way up there in the announcer's box! A real good question, old timer."[164]

Ted really wanted to do something for Saul, to help him get around. Sarah said Saul couldn't handle a car, so Ted asked, "What about a bike?" With the bad leg, though, that wouldn't work either. Ted probably sent some money from time to time. Saul passed away a couple of years later, a loner, and was put to rest beside his mother and his sister May on a quiet hillside in Goleta, California. Chaz Venzor tells how Ted always asked after his Aunt Sarah, too. "Two or three years ago, while Sarah was still living – she's the last of the

Venzors – Ted would always call up, call Dee and say, 'You make sure you let me know if there's anything she needs.'"[165]

This author asked Ted about Saul Venzor in April 2000. "Saul was a damn good athlete," Ted answered. "He was my mother's brother. He had a little bottle problem; he couldn't handle things. He was a pretty good baseball player. Santa Barbara. I don't know any other relatives that had that much ability."[166]

Sarah Venzor Diaz   (February 10, 1905 - November 3, 1999)

Sarah was born in 1905 in Santa Barbara in an adobe-style house with a dirt floor. When Sarah's birth certificate was filled out, her name was left off. Apparently, the Venzors wanted a girl named Sarah; it was understood that two previous stillborn children had been intended to bear the name. Perhaps they'd been reluctant to fill in the name on the certificate. Many years later, she had to add her own name "Sarah Venzor." This Sarah stuck, and lived to be 94 years old.

She told me about her life and the family background. The one time I interviewed Sarah, it was at length. As far as I know, I'm the only writer to have interviewed her – Ted Williams' aunt – and she had a lot to say. Some might find her comments a bit rambling, but there was a real charm to her way of speaking and I fortunately just let her talk. A portion of her commentary is provided here, and it touches on several points, many of which she went into in more depth after I asked follow-up questions. Let me provide a bit of what she had to say, without interruption. As we saw above, her father was a shepherd and there were a number of dairymen, stonemasons, and bricklayers among her uncles.

"To cross the border, you had to have so much money to come into the United States in those days. When my brother was just about a year old, my father decided to come to California, to cross the border to Texas – El Paso – and then to come to California. My uncles...my grandma had 14 children. Fourteen children. When she married my grandfather, her first pregnancy she had twins, but one died at birth. After that, she had 13. The last pregnancy, she had twins again. One of them passed away. I didn't know some of my uncles. They stayed in Texas."

After May and Sam Williams moved to San Diego, Sarah took the opportunity to visit and stay for a prolonged period. "I took care of Ted," she told me. "I was going to high school and I was about 17. I should have graduated when I was 18, the following year. Santa Barbara was a small, Spanish town, and I thought, well, I wanted to go to San Diego and take care of Ted and Danny, his brother.

"I am 13 years older than Ted. I'm 94 years old, and he's 80 right now. Oh, Ted is a wonderful person! Oh my gosh, you talk to Ted and he looks you straight in the eye. He knows whether you're telling the truth or not. He can always tell. A wonderful person. He's been wonderful to me. I love Ted. And Danny.

"I went to San Diego and I took care of Teddy and Danny. Coming from a small school to go to a big school like in San Diego – San Diego is beautiful – I was interested in the Salvation Army. I was interested in becoming an officer, too, like May. May was very devoted. Spreckels, you know, the sugar manufacturer, he's the one who gave May that home at 4121 Utah. (The wealthy businessman – John D. Spreckels – effectively donated the house to May Williams in support of her devoted efforts for the Salvation Army.)

Sarah talked about Danny, and how he never could measure up to Ted, so he acted out his frustrations in a number of stunts or through delinquency. We will look more at Danny Williams later on. After he got married, though, he would visit Sarah and the family in Santa Barbara. "He used to come and visit us, Danny. And his two boys. He called his two boys Ted and Sam. Ted put them through college and one of them learned to play the guitar beautiful. He was auditioning in L.A. He came by and he had a girl. He said that was his wife. When Danny passed away, his wife remarried right away. She married a chiropractor, but I don't know his name. Just up north some place. Her name was Jean. They moved some place up north."[167] (Jean did indeed marry a chiropractor named Dave Barber. He lived in Fresno and, interestingly, also ran a folk music coffeehouse there in the very early 1960s called The Renaissance. Danny's son Sam was inspired by the music around him.) "A lot of times the different people who were playing there would end up at our house." Sam remembers his grandmother May playing piano and guitar. "I don't know that I ever remember her playing trumpet, although I know that she did. Cornet. I play cornet also. And she sang, too. I'm not a great singer, but I sang some. I made my

Sarah Venzor with sister May, both Salvationists.

living at it for 10 years. A singer-songwriter. I started out playing in a band. Whatever was in the Top Ten, playing bars. A lot of colleges. From Port Angeles, Washington down through California. Pretty much up and down the coast. Mostly solo. Occasionally some duos and trios. Sometimes I would be forced to work regular jobs. Some of everything. Restaurants. Bar tending. A couple of summers, tomato harvesting here. When I turned 30 I pretty much decided it was time to give it up ."[168]

May's sister continued, "Sam was a photographer there in San Diego, but he wasn't much of a businessman; I don't know. She had to get out and sell the *War Cry*. She used to get just so much for every *War Cry* that she sold, but she was the world's champion *War Cry* seller."[169]

"Ted was about 4 years old. Danny was just a baby. I met this fellow, so I stayed in San Diego. I started selling *War Cry*s and helping May. I quit high school. I couldn't cope with such a big school. Every time I'd go to a different class, I'd get lost. I wouldn't know where I was. As long as I could, I stuck it out but I couldn't take it. I was failing in my classes. I couldn't find my class and the kids were rushing around, rushing you here and there and bumping into you and everything with your books, and I didn't know where my locker was...oh heavens! I just quit. And then I started selling *War Cry*s and helping my sister and taking care of Teddy and Danny.

"I was the flower girl at May's wedding, when she married Sam Williams. I was just a little girl. When they were married here in Santa Barbara, I was her flower girl. May was born in 1891. My mother has nine children. Two passed away when they were born. There was Pete and May and Mary and Daniel – that's the one who was in World War I; he lies in Flanders Field in France. [He died when he was] 23 years old. He was the one who was taking care of us, supporting us because my father was beginning to fail them, his health. Daniel was the one who was helping us. Then my brother Saul was born in 1903. He was a ballplayer, too. He played for the Pacific League in those days. He was a good hitter, too. The first time he went to bat, he played the Foresters and other leagues here in the South Pacific, but then he was interested in a girl and he didn't want to leave town so he just forgot baseball. He turned to pool."

May was 12 years older than her younger sister Sarah, and Sarah looked up to May. Wanting to follow May's example, Sarah also joined the Salvation Army.

"I've had a wonderful, interesting life myself. I went to the Salvation Army Training College when I went to San Diego. I met a fellow who was in the Navy. He was from Michigan, Big Rapids, Michigan. Chester Amidon. And I had a son. Now I have eight grandchildren and 16 great-grandchildren, and now I have three great-great-grandchildren. I've had a very interesting life. But being in the Salvation Army...I was a home girl. I couldn't be away from my mother, and I had my little boy. We had to travel. Salvation Army people send you. You don't go where you want to go. They send you wherever they want you to go, where they think you'll be fitted for the city and for the work that we do in the Salvation Army. We were sent to Santa Ana and then to Pomona, and then we were sent to Salt Lake City and that's where my son was born. Well, that was too far away from home. Then from there, I came on a visit to Santa Barbara. Oh heavens, I didn't want to go back, but I had to. After my vacation here, I went back to Salt Lake. From there, we were sent to Thermopolis, Wyoming and then I just couldn't take it any more. I came home."

She and Chester Amidon separated. "I remarried after I don't know how many years. My husband [Arnold Diaz] was a musician. He had a mariachi band. He was an immigrant from Mexico. His father was wounded in the war in Mexico. In the operation, he passed away. He gave his boy, my husband Arnold, to his brother. So his uncle raised him, and then they crossed the border way up in Matagorda. They went to Texas and then in 1917, Arnold joined the army, the military army, because there was a war in 1918. He was sent to France. He didn't go to fight. They put him in the medical corps. They had their band in the army, and they used to go and entertain in the camps. Wherever there was a camp, they'd go and entertain them with their music, so he never got to see any...but he saw a lot in France. A lot of French girls. Then he came to Santa Barbara. That was in 1921 or 22, I guess. I met him just from across the street. We used to talk to each other. Then I left for San Diego, and I didn't come home for about four or five years. I came back to get married to Amidon. He had gotten married [Arnold] and he had two children. That was in 1923 and then I got married here. My son was born in 1925. I left the Salvation Army because I couldn't take the traveling around. I was too far from home when I went to Salt Lake and Thermopolis, and my mother here with my brothers and my sisters. So I came home.

"My brothers bought a home for my mother here in Santa Barbara. I've lived in this home for 77 years. Ted would come up and visit when he could. That's when he would play ball with my brothers. The one that played ball with the Pacific League here, that was Saul. He was two years older than I was. When Ted would come, the first thing they would do is get out there in the field and pitch to each other, throw the ball to each other, and bat to each other. Out in the field. We always had a garden. We were poor. We always had a garden, though, and raised chickens. We grew vegetables and fruit trees. We always had plenty to eat. As I look back now, I can see I've been through I don't know how many depressions. That was terrible.

"When we used to go visit in San Diego, he [Ted] was just a young boy. My brother had a Model T Ford or a Model A Ford, and we used to go to San Diego. Right away, Ted would want to drive the car and go and hunt. He loved to hunt. He loved to fish. My father, too. My father was a good fisherman. And my brothers all used to go out here on the wharf in Santa Barbara and fish. And my father."

"I'm still a Salvationist, but I don't get out very much because I have no way of going. I have to have someone take me. I still am a Salvationist. I'm a good Christian. I try. I try very much. Ted, of course, that rubbed off on him. He's very generous. He saw to that little Jimmy Fund. I never forget that, how he'd go out every year and raise money to support little children that were poor and had no way of getting treated. He loved his children. That's one thing about Ted. He loves people. Of course, he was a little cocky. I have a picture where, finally, they said, Ted takes off his hat to this audience when he played ball. I don't have a real picture. I have it from the newspaper. I live here alone.

"I don't remember if I ever talked with May about Ted's work with the Jimmy Fund, but she knew. She called him 'Precious.' Everybody was 'Precious' to May. She was a very devoted Christian woman. That little rascal of Danny. He would do anything to attract attention. That was in him. I think he was envious that Ted could do everything. Everything was Ted. Everything Danny did was wrong. He was a little scoundrel. May could never say a bad word, you know, a cuss word. All she'd call him, if she talked to my mother or talking about Danny, 'He's a scoundrel. He's a rascal,' she'd call him. But never a real bad word.

"She was very proud of Ted. They used to call her up and tell her, 'May, turn on your TV. Ted's on playing ball.' Oh, and then she'd start praying, to have him make a home run. I did, too, when I used to see him play. We used to see him play at the games here in L.A. One time my sister and I went to the back gate and we told one of the ballplayers there to call Ted. We were new at going to ballgames. We used to go and see my older brother Saul play, too, here when the Foresters would come or when they'd play here at the ball field in Santa Barbara. But in L.A., a big game, we went to the gate and we told one ballplayer, 'Would you please call Ted Williams? Tell him his two aunts are here to see him.' Oh my gosh, one ballplayer says, 'Oh, no! Not me!' Everybody used to go and call him. They'd say they were related and that they were friends or they were relations, and they wanted to talk to Ted. When Ted would go [to see who was calling on him], it wasn't [a relative at all]. It was somebody looking for money or asking for help – it wasn't true. After that he told them – the other ballplayers – he told them, 'Never call me.' They knew. They wouldn't, because he'd get mad. Well, that was kind of rude to have people go and say you were related just to get to talk to him and then find out that they're just looking for a handout.

"May didn't follow baseball really, because she was too busy trying to make a living. But she was interested. When she'd know he was on TV, there she was, just rooting for him. 'Lord, help him to make a home run!'"[170] San Diego newspaperman Forrest Warren, a neighborhood friend and a member of the Salvation Army Advisory Board, said that as Ted started breaking major baseball records May herself "became an ardent baseball enthusiast." Warren seems to be the only one who reported this kind of transformation, but he did document one touching moment during the 1946 All-Star Game. "I called her on the telephone to ask, 'Are you tuned in, May? Teddy is playing.' 'Yes, I'm sitting by my radio, praying for Teddy to get one good hit.' While we were talking there came more than an answer to a mother's prayer. It was his first home run. 'Thank God, my prayer was answered,' and she hung up the receiver."[171]

"[Ted] took care of May [by sending money.] I took care of my sister when she had her sickness. She came here to live with me. She spent her last few years with me. Everybody was 'Precious' to her. She'd go out -- our neighbors all had children and she'd go out with the guitar and sing to them. Salvation Army songs."

Salvation Army group: Sarah standing, far right, May to her left.

Sarah knew that Ted had suffered a couple of strokes and was having a rough time of it. It made her weep to think of him incapacitated, but Ted was on the phone asking what *he* could do for *her*.

"Ted, poor thing, I remember his birthday, so I always send him a card. Sometimes maybe on Christmas, but mostly on his birthday. I talked to Ted. He talks good, bless his heart, but all I did was cry. I just feel for him, being as sick as he is. He's talked to my doctor. He's very much interested in trying to see what he can do for me. He's really been wonderful.

"You tell Ted you talked to me, his Aunt Sarah. Bless his heart. Thank you for calling me. I hope you can understand how I feel. I wish they had this in writing. I don't know why they always bring up his Mexican heritage. I know that a lot of writers don't like him. He's a wonderful person. Of course, he was cocky. He wouldn't put his hat off his head to his people, and then he finally did. But he meant well. He loved his children. He still loved, but they couldn't understand why he was never home. But then he had to have a rest! He had to get away from that work that he was doing, I mean with baseball."[172]

In September 1960, Sarah Diaz watched Ted's last game on television. Manuel Herrera, referring to Sarah as "Mom," remembers the day with clarity: "It was September and fall was in the air and the game was on television. I had just finished eating breakfast and I was sitting in the living room watching the TV, the Boston Red Sox and the Baltimore Orioles. The announcer was Curt Gowdy, the voice of the Sox. I called Mom to the front room to watch the game; needless to say the Red Sox were and still are her team! Well, Curt Gowdy was really giving Ted the big attention before the game, and he said "Retirement." Mom said, "Wait till he get up to the plate." She still had her kitchen apron on. Well, Ted came up and gave one a ride in the fifth against Jack Fisher the right-handed pitcher. Curt Gowdy said, "A cold damp day kept it from going out." In the eighth he got hold of one. I looked at Mom and she had her eyes closed; she was praying for a homer. I couldn't believe it, he drove it out of Fenway like a shot. The next thing I knew, she was crying and said, "Atta boy, Ted! I was praying for him" – and he did it with a bang. Mom said, "I told you he would hit it out." I told Mom, "He didn't tip his hat. Just like a stubborn Venzor, hits one out and no hat tip." She was

Sarah and Carmen Ponce, cousins.

so happy that her nephew finished with a bang. I was crying just as she was. It was a special day at the little house redwood house at 1008 Chino Street."[173]

Aaron Paul Venzor (June 22, 1907 - August 2, 1980)

Paul Venzor was the whole thing wrapped up in one: a cowboy, baseball player and longshoreman.

The Venzors had to work hard to make ends meet. Sarah Diaz told Manuel that Pete, Daniel, Paul and Saul all slept in the same bed as she did. "We all slept in the same bed, Manuel, and each one of us down the line would say, 'Good night, Mom, I love you' when we went to bed."[174]

Paul married Tillie Andrade and they had three children: Rosalie Larson, Frank Venzor, and Carolyn O'Grady. Paul became a Catholic in marriage, one of the few Catholics in the family. Teresa Cordero Contreras was baptized Catholic, and attended Mass at 8 a.m. – but then walked down the street and attended Protestant Sunday school with her mother Mary at 9:30 at the Calvary Baptist Church.[175]

Initially, Paul was hired by his older brother Pete and worked on the Tecolote Ranch in Goleta for many years. Paul's son Frank says, "We're a bunch of cowboys. We really are a bunch of cowboys from the ranch. Spaulding was involved with Gene Autry, the singing cowboy. My dad used to take me to Tex Ritter. My dad broke horses. He was actually a cowhand, a cowboy. He worked on the ranch for maybe 10 years. After that, he went to be a longshoreman. A stevedore."[176]

Rozie Larson characterizes her father as a "quiet and passive person." Paul and Tillie lived at the Tecolote Ranch, and Paul "had a great love for horses. He helped groom the horses and helped the trainers at the ranch. The Spauldings would have big rodeos, and famous dignitaries from all over California would attend. Will Rogers was a frequent visitor. I remember my father saying that he got to ride Will's horse, which was a thrill for him. Ted and his brother Dan were frequent visitors, too."

Paul particularly loved to take part in the fiestas, working with horses from the Spaulding stable. "During our annual Santa Barbara Fiesta parades, Dad would drive a team of horses hauling the Fiesta dancers, or he would ride the Palomino horses in their silver splendor."

"We lived at the ranch for several years before moving back to Santa Barbara. The family ran into hard times. During the Depression, my father was able to find employment as a golf caddy at the San Ysidro Ranch. (Guests didn't have golf carts back then.) When Bing Crosby golfed at the ranch, my dad would caddy for him and other celebrities who were guests at San Ysidro.

"During World War II, he was employed at Port Hueneme as a longshoreman, becoming a foreman. He worked during and after the war, until his injury. He was on a ship loading big steel pillars, which broke loose and crushed his ankle."[177]

Even after the Depression, war, and the debilitating injury, Paul enjoyed a good rapport with horses. "My dad had a way with horses," Rozie wrote me. "He could calm the wildest horses. My sister and I had rented horses from a nearby stable, and one of the horses got spooked. We were having a heck of a time. Being we were close to home, we stopped to have our dad help us with this unruly horse. Dad got on the horse, did four steps back, and a couple of circles. The horse gave a couple of kicks, but he calmed the horse down and walked the horse down the block. It didn't give us any more trouble, but of course, we returned to the stables A.S.A.P."[178]

Paul was one of the ballplayers in the family, along with Saul and Bruno, and played on teams in Santa Barbara.

Without the ability to work, Paul became tormented by the scourge of alcoholism. It cost him his marriage, and more. Manuel Herrera minces no words in talking of his Uncle Paul. "Paul Venzor was such a wino that he didn't need to be embalmed when they buried the bum; he was so pickled that he stunk! He was what they termed 'rum dumb' and the drink got him. He once drank rubbing alcohol and had to have his stomach pumped. He turned out to be the worst of the lot and still lived longer than his brothers!"

Manuel added, "Mom [Sarah] was the silent leader of the Venzor family. When Saul and Paul lost their marriages, they fell apart and the kids really suffered. With their drinking problems, Saul and Paul, she took the time to put her brothers in a state mental hospital to dry out. If it wasn't for Mom, her brothers would have died in the streets of Santa Barbara, California. That is how really bad off her brothers were! Bruno cared less and Jean was just as bad with the drink 'til she became a Christian again."[179]

"Mom [Sarah] truly loved her family and she stood by them so darn often, and was always a force in their personal lives. When their own families gave up on her brothers, she took her cross and still marched on and never once changed her mind. I remember when Saul wanted to quit the wine, Mom took him down to Camarillo State Hospital so he could get help and 'dry out' of his addiction. It didn't help at all. The poor man was at it again as soon after he came home! Heck, we pulled Paul Venzor out of a little apartment in Watts down in the L.A. area. I will never forget Mom knocking on the apartment door and then she opening it and seeing her brother in bed going through the DT's. Mom hurried into the room and helped Paul as I looked on. He was in bad shape. She asked Paul if he wanted help and he acknowledged yes, so we got him into Camarillo State hospital as well. Paul became what people call, 'rum dumb' – he lost his sense of thinking or as we say today 'fried his brains' with wine. I think he lived to be about 70 years of age, but I still can't believe he stayed alive so long with all the abuse he dealt to himself."[180]

Growing up in the family, there would often be one adventure or another. Paul's son Frank remembers, "My dad took me to the air show at Goleta and we watched this guy jump out of an airplane, a paratrooper. They loved to fly airplanes. Goddamn, they used to love to fly airplanes! My uncle and my cousins, they rented an airplane. My cousin Sooky [Joe Moreno, Jeanne Venzor's son] had a pilot's license. He was a fighter, a scrapper. A biker. He was short, a good-looking guy, called the 'Mexican Marlon Brando.' It was around the beginning of the Korean War, they rented an airplane and they all piled in. Sooky was in charge and he was driving it and, man, they were diving at the house, over the hill at Chino Street. It was me and Manuel and Natalie. We were watching them and I could see who it was, the airplane came so low to the ground. They were all nuts."[181]

Paul Venzor and Tillie Andrade Venzor.

Social Security records have him listed as Aaron Venzor, and so does the California birth index, but his gravestone has him as Paul Aaron Venzor. His daughter Rozie informs me that his first name was indeed the Biblical name Aaron. Paul Venzor covered a lot of ground in his life, as his gravestone inscription reminds us. It reads, "A cowboy, baseball player, golfer, longshoreman, grandpa and our dad." It's a good bet that a good portion of the men in America would love an inscription along those lines.

Bruno Venzor   (October 6, 1909 - June 23, 1974)

Bruno was perhaps the uncle Ted was closest to, the youngest brother among the Venzors. Less intimidating than his brother Saul the taskmaster (and not the ballplayer Saul was, either), Bruno nonetheless loved the game and played when he could. Manuel saw him pitch once in an old-timers game at Cabrillo Park in Santa Barbara. "Bruno threw a knuckleball with little effectiveness and his fast ball was even worse, but he laughed all the time on the mound 'til Saul – who was the first baseman – got fed up with his pitching and pulled him out of the game. Saul always wanted to win and Bruno always was ready to laugh at any given opportunity."[182] Saul may have inspired Ted more, and helped provide the drive and determination necessary to become a great ballplayer, but it sounds like Ted and Bruno enjoyed each other more.

One thing they shared was a love of fishing. Both Saul and Bruno fished, but Saul was exceptionally strict. Bruno was a little more happy-go-lucky by contrast, and he had his own small boat. "The man could drink a case of beer and fish like all get-out and he knew the current in the channel like a salt captain." Manuel recalls a time when there were four kids out on a boat with Bruno and the fog rolled in. He asked the kids if they knew how to get back to the dock. "We all pointed in different directions and he laughed at us. He said, 'Look at the current, you dummies; that alone will tell you the way home.' Shucks, we didn't have a clue as to what was happening.

"Uncle Bruno would show up at Stearns Wharf while me and my buddies were fishing. Bruno would put on a show with a bamboo pole and snag hooks; he caught his fish with no bait just five plain hooks and 3 or 4 shiners at a time. Soon a crowd showed up and he would have a ball with all the attention, and he would ask me if I wanted to go fishing on his boat, *Some Tub*. I said, yeah, and off to Naples Point we went where he knew the fishing grounds. It was usually sea bass or sheephead but my Dad's favorite was red snapper and that was easy to catch. He liked halibut and so did I. After fishing, he stopped at the Cliff Room for a cold one. My cousin said he would toss his catch on the bar so everyone could see, a real character. He told me he taught Ted how to drive after he hit the home run in the PCL Championship. They were headed for quail hunting out in the Borrego Mountains and Bruno taught him how to drive on the way out after the game."[183]

Bruno may have also taught Ted the curve ball. Dee Allen says that Saul refused to show Ted the curve when Ted was around 10. It could ruin his arm, Saul told him - a good point. Bruno showed Ted a few tips, though. Ted may also have helped Saul earn a little bit of money on the side during informal ball games, collecting wagers from opposing players and from spectators.[184]

Happy-go-lucky that Bruno may have been at times, and despite sharing neighboring houses on Chino Street, Manuel says of his uncles, "There were a cold lot and Bruno was always mad and upset about everything. They were not the close and kind family my aunt told me they had been." He recalls one time when he and Uncle Paul had worked all day on Bruno's retaining wall between his property at 1006 Chino and the adjoining ones. Paul lived at 1002 Chino Street. When Bruno came home, he ripped the wall down and told Paul to stay on his side and leave his work alone.[185]

Bruno's wife Marian (Romero) cleaned houses, and Bruno drove a cement mixer. Though he worked some on the ranch, and worked in construction, his primary job was transporting cement for Southern Pacific Milling and another Santa Barbara company.

He loved to dress up western style in a white cowboy hat and western pants and boots, and parade with the Elks Club. Bruno also played snare drum for the Elks drum and bugle corps. Bruno's wife Marian termed it the "Drunk Corps" since the group often repaired to quench their post-parade thirst. Bruno was dubbed the "Sheriff of Chino Street" by Sarah's husband Arnold Diaz, and he loved the moniker.

He was very proud of his nephew Ted Williams and called him a "top notcher" at baseball. Bruno named his own son after his older brother Daniel, who was killed in the first World War. He wanted Danny to become a baseball star like Ted Williams, but it just wasn't to be.

Danny Venzor remembered, "My dad played baseball. My Uncle Saul -- he was Dee's dad – he was very much in baseball, and he was offered a contract when he was real young to play for Seattle, and he turned it down for some unknown reason. I remember when Ted was managing the Senators, when they were playing out here, playing the Angels. He would come up there and get tickets for my son David -- who just passed away in February – my dad would pick up my son. He must have been 10 or 11 years old and they would go down to where Ted was staying, at the Royal Hotel or one of the hotels down there. I remember my son saying, 'Ted just can't sit down!' He made him nervous. Walking over to the TV, changing channels, sit-

Bruno Venzor on *Some Tub.*

ting down and getting up, looking out the window…." I said, 'Well, David, you've got to realize he's the manager of a major league baseball team and he's got all these things on his mind. The pitchers, the baseball club, his lineup and all that.' I explained that. 'Well, he can't sit down.' Bruno spoke to Ted like an uncle asking something of a nephew, "I want to sit in the dugout!" Danny explains, "My dad always talked to Ted like that – to tell him what he wanted him to do. Ted replied, "No, Bruno. I can't. I can't do that." Ted got them good box seats, right next to the visitors' dugout."[186]

Bruno Venzor.

"When his mother died, he stayed at the Santa Barbara Inn. He only wanted to see my dad and, before the funeral, to take him out to the cemetery. So we went over there in the morning. He had just gotten out of the shower. He was exercising. He had a bat, you know, and he kind of used the bat to exercise. He'd take a couple of swings. He'd see his reflection in the window overlooking the beach. Then he orders breakfast for the three of us. He was under a fictitious name, because he didn't want anybody bugging him.

"At the get-together, at the barbecue it was very interesting. He had some very good memory of games, and ballplayers and different incidents. I asked him about Eddie Mathews. I played ball with Eddie in high school, in Santa Barbara. Eddie made the big leagues for Milwaukee. Yeah, he knew Eddie. He said Eddie was going to be a Hall of Famer - which he turned out to be. He was really interesting to talk to.

"At one point in time, I wanted to be a ballplayer. When I got out of the service, I had to go to Korea. That kind of halted that. I didn't see him, but he was there. I was in the 981st, the Army, a National Guard artillery battalion.

We went to Japan and then went to Korea. When I got out I went to City College and I played semipro. I never got exposure. It's all in the timing. I was always active in sports all my life. Probably with Ted as a cousin, it made me want to go into baseball."[187]

Bruno loved baseball but wasn't a star player. He was fast and played infield, and even after Saul couldn't play any more, Bruno kept on, playing with industrial league, semipro teams. For his part, Danny Venzor played on the same team as his Santa Barbara High School mate Eddie Mathews, and went to the championship. A couple of years earlier, Saul had called Ted and said he was going to start a semipro team and needed some equipment. Shortly thereafter, some large cardboard cartons arrived and there were bats from every member of the Boston Red Sox – Doerr, Pesky and so forth, and four Ted Williams bats. Bruno kept the gloves, baseballs and bats under Danny's bed at his home at 1006 Chino Street. Danny asked Saul for one of the bats, and was told, "You can pick out any bat except a Ted Williams bat." He took a Bobby Doerr model, but Bruno told him, "Don't ever use it. You can put it up on the wall in your room." In 1949, Santa Barbara was up against San Diego for the C.I.F. championship, the same tournament Ted Williams had starred in 13 years earlier. The game was scheduled for Lane Field, and Danny snuck the bat down. It must have had some major league hits in it, because the first time up, Danny hit a ball about 400 feet to right center that bounced up against the wall, just missing going out. Danny got a triple out of it. Mathews hit one out later in the game, but Santa Barbara lost that one."

Bruno worked hard to mold Danny into a ballplayer. "All the time! Jeezus! My dad just hammered, hammered, hammered into me. At Chino Street, it's kind of an asphalt street and it rolled down. I'd come home from practice. He's got his bat and a ball. He'd say, 'Get the glove.' We'd be about 30 feet away. Pepper. He'd bang them. He'd bang them. And if missed the goddamn ball, the goddamn ball would run all the way down the end of the street, and he'd say, 'Run! Run! Run!' I'd get the ball, and 'Run! Run! Run!' back, you know. Then just to get a rest, I'd throw the ball right at his goddamn head.

We had a bank in the back, a hill at the end of the street. I'd throw the ball right at his head, just to give me a rest.

"My dad, since we were in grammar school, junior high and especially Eddie's dad, my dad and him would always go to the games, even though we're down at Ventura, or Oxnard or up north. We're talking like a 50-mile radius or something like that, and they would drive together and they would critique. They were pretty close, and they both drank. They would take a jug up there, sit in the car watching the game and take some nips out of there."

Danny enjoyed the Breakfast of Champions, too. Ted had signed an endorsement contract with Wheaties, and received more samples than he could eat, so he had huge cartons of the individual serving sizes sent to his relatives in Santa Barbara. "I remember as kids, we used to get like 1000 little boxes of Wheaties. The whole family grew up - the kids all grew up - with Wheaties coming out of our ears."[188]

Danny was good, but ended up being shipped off to Korea for two years, and that interruption hurt. He was back from Korea before his famous uncle arrived there. Many years later, Danny visited Fort Pendleton to play golf with a friend who had re-upped and eventually become a full bird colonel.

B. P. O. E. 613 Elks Drum and Bugle Corps, Santa Barbara.

He went in the mess hall, and there were all these 8 foot by 10 foot photographs of honored Marines. General after general – and Lee Trevino and Ted Williams.

Bruno may have thought he knew a little more about baseball than maybe he did. Manuel told a story about Bruno and himself visiting Ted at a ballgame.

"If you wanted to know Ted, you had better search him out. He had a different lifestyle than us folks. I took it upon myself with to head down to Anaheim and see if I could locate Ted at the game that evening. My wife and I enjoyed the game and then I had a brainstorm, why not give a note to the usher telling him that his cousin was a spectator and would like to see Ted after the game. It was a big chance, but what the hell? I really had nothing to lose -- or did I? The usher was very kind and suggested that I wait for Ted at the rear of the stadium where the bus was waiting to take the Rangers to LAX.

"Old Ted got the message and he wanted to know, 'Where in hell is my so-and-so cousin, and who in the hell is my cousin?' I said, 'I am over here, Ted.' Then he recognized me and I introduced him to my wife and I had to answer all his family questions. It took some quick thinking to remember all the people he wanted to know about, mostly Saul, Bruno, Sarah, and Jeanne or Jenny as he called her. He promised to call and keep in touch, and I told him the family would be coming to see his team play. He gave me a number and it was for tickets for the whole family. They were box seats, right behind the Rangers dugout on the first base side.

"The family got all my news and they were amazed about the invitation, so we planned a trip to enjoy a game and see the hero of the family. It was Mom [Sarah] and Arnold, Bruno, Jenny and me. Just the five of us. Mom drove and I must tell you she didn't drive over 55 miles an hour in her whole life. I was getting nervous because I thought we would never make it by game time. It turns out we got there very early. Mom had the wrong start time by two hours. So I suggested we drive to the front of the stadium, get the start time and ask when the gates were to open up.

"Just then, the Rangers charter bus is heading right toward us, heading in to the stadium, and I tell Mom. Uncle Bruno yells, 'Block the bus! The bus, get right in front of the damn thing, Sarah!' Mom followed her brother's orders, the loyal Venzor that she was. Bruno got out of the car from the back seat, and guess who was in the front seat of the bus cursing to no end? And he was motioning to head for the stadium and get the hell out of the way. I was laughing. Bruno jumped back into his seat and we drove to the stadium parking lot and picked up our 'call waiting tickets ' at the window for friends and family.

"I had a chance to talk with Nellie Fox. He was a coach for Ted. Mom asked Nellie if he could get Ted to come over and see his Aunt Sarah, but Nellie said, 'Lady, nobody bothers Ted when he is taking infield with the team.' Nellie was not going to get in Dutch with Ted. It was an unwritten rule; you don't bother Ted when he is working with the team.

"We did have a chance to see Ted before the game, but the fans were very rude. Mom and Jenny were first, then Bruno and Arnold and myself. It was a beautiful day for a game and Ted had to tell the fans, 'Please let me visit with my family, then I will sign your autographs, just please wait.' It worked for a while, but then more fans showed up. Old Ted was more popular than the players on his team! No joke!

"Then Pop [Arnold] had an idea for Ted. While they were talking, he was signing autographs, Arnold suggested that Ted get a stamp with his name on it and use that instead of signing his name so damn much. Hell, there was no need to sign your name that often, Ted! Ted told him that he tried that idea and the first two autograph seekers looked at Ted after he stamped his name on their programs. They wanted to know why Ted couldn't write his name, did he break his arm or just what happened, where was he hurting? The kids ripped up the programs right in front of Ted and walked away mad. Ted told Arnold, 'You have to hand-sign your name, no way around it!' Now it is a very big business!

"Uncle Bruno had told me that he coached the local Elks service team to a championship and if Ted needed help he would be right there. He knew from experience that a manager needed all the help he could get and since he was Ted's uncle, who better to volunteer some good ole Venzor help? After all, he won the Santa Barbara Junior League Championship out of 18 teams. Well we parked and got box seats and I began to get nervous. Uncle Bruno still wanted to send an ear full of advice to Ted. I tried to talk him out of it, saying that Nellie Fox and John Roseboro knew a little about the game, and that Ted had 17 years experience of major league baseball under his belt. After five beers and three bags of peanuts, though, Uncle Bruno was ready to give the Thumper some badly needed advice.

"Uncle Bruno told Ted, 'I had a Championship Junior League Baseball Team in Santa Barbara, and I want to tell you how you [Ted] should run your team.' I told Bruno to please not say those words, but he insisted and Ted gave him some choice words in return! Ted told Bruno, 'You see that seat I got you? Take your ass and put the damn thing back there!' I laughed as Uncle Bruno headed back to his seat. He felt Ted just didn't understand what he needed to know. My words were, 'Uncle Bruno, please let it die!'

"After the game I was given orders to follow the Rangers charter bus to the airport for their flight. I suggested no, but Uncle Bruno had too many beers and was not making a wise decision, this event I tried to talk him out of! Between him needing a bathroom and the charter, oh boy! Well, we made it to the parking area and there was Ted with the owner discussing the game, Uncle Bruno got out of my car and a long arm came out of Ted's side and Ted yelled, 'Bruno, get in that car and go the hell home.' That was my final visit to the Big A and the Texas Rangers with Uncle Bruno. He embarrassed the hell out of me."[189]

Bruno was a favorite of Ted's, though, despite it all, and when he wanted to call Santa Barbara, he always called on Bruno's phone and not Sarah's. "He never got the number right for some reason," Manuel recalls.[190]

One of Ted's last visits to San Diego was in 1992. He stopped by Santa Barbara for a family barbeque. Danny Venzor said, "The last time he was here was after the time when his mom died. He was here with his son John-Henry, when they had the All-Star Game down there in San Diego. He was honored down there. They had some of his old cronies. They had the ceremonies and they named the freeway or something after him. He stopped by here on his way down to San Diego and we had a big family barbecue and get-together."[191]

Jeanne Venzor Winet   (June 26, 1912 - February 4, 1986)

Jeanne was the youngest child. Aunt Jeanne, or Jenny as Ted called her, was a full 19 years younger than her big sister May Venzor Williams. She was just six years older than her nephew Ted. Joe Villarino told Leigh Montville that his older brother was even going to marry Jeanne at one point.[192]

She married Joseph Moreno, and they had two children – Alberta (Abby) Moreno and her brother Joseph (Sooky) Moreno, Joe Jr. The nickname Sooky was given by his Aunt Sarah, taken from a comic strip character in the local newspaper. "He was short for a male," Manuel Herrera said, "and had a complex with that stigma. He was quick to fight, but always suffered a lot and made a fool out of himself as well. He was a character and liked the bar action, if you know what I mean. Remember that Jeanne was a Venzor and she married about two or three times, but Alberta was her only girl and Joe (Sooky) was her only real son. Her second marriage was to a Jewish man named Maurice Winet."[193]

Most of what I know about Jeanne Venzor comes from an interview with Dr. Howard Winet, a professor of orthopedic surgery in the biomedical engineering department at UCLA. He works in biomaterials, in tissue engineering. He is also Jeanne's stepson.

"My father's name was Maurice, and he was Jeanne's second husband. She was number four of my father's five wives. I was 12 or 13 and I'm now 65, so it was around 1950. When they got divorced, I was away at college. I think it was the early 60s when the divorce took place.

"She had a daughter and a son. Abby and Joe. Everybody called him Sooky. Joe didn't talk much about his father. There was also an adopted daughter – Mary – who was the Catholic of the family, and she was around the age of Abby so it was almost like they were twin sisters."[194] Mary the adopted girl, "the Catholic of the family," was Mary Redding, one of Manuel Herrera's sisters.

"Sooky was older. He was a bit of a Romeo – actually, he was a gang member. I got a real education. When I came out here, I didn't know anything. I was really a bumpkin. I was from the West Side of Chicago, so I wasn't totally innocent, but Joe was the source of....In fact, the first Spanish I learned was all cuss words, and I learned them from Joe.

"It was the gang that came after the Pachucos. The Pachucos were born in World War II and a little bit after. There was this transition and the Pachucos no longer dominated and there was a whole bunch of other gangs. It was almost like a Balkanization of the gang culture, if you will.

"Sooky was in Camarillo. He was in detention. I think the story was he pulled a knife on a cop. He was stealing something from a grocery store. This was after he came back from the Air Force. They were stationed in Greenland, but after he came home from that he got into the gangs. I don't have a clear memory of the whole story now. Prison, yes. We had to go up and get him out of Camarillo.

"We lived in Bellflower, California. For part of the marriage, I lived in Santa Barbara, and for a couple of months I lived on the little farm where Arnold and Sarah were, a little farm up on Chino Street.

"Jeanne was a beauty operator. She always spelled it Jeanne. I never knew her by any other name. Nor can I remember any document with 'Jean' on it. And poor writing was no excuse. She had excellent handwriting.

"Winet is a derived name. My Uncle Bob changed his name during World War II, and my father followed him. My father's reason was the reason of many people of Eastern European extraction – there was prejudice in the military service. People changed their names so that they wouldn't be identified with the group that they thought was being discriminated against. It was Winetski, and they just knocked off the "ski."

"We moved from Chino Street to State Street in Santa Barbara, right on State Street. You could hear the traffic and everything. And we lived right in the beauty parlor. We were in the back and Jeanne had her shop in the front.

"My father was a medic in the Pacific during the war, but there still was an aircraft industry after the war making aircraft for the burgeoning public – civil aircraft development. The airlines were starting to boom and they needed planes. He worked for Douglas. He worked for Hughes. He was a quality control engineer in the aircraft industry. Not a real engineer like a college graduate type engineer, but in those days, you got a lot of on the job training.

"We moved on to Bellflower from there. She had a shop there, too, but it wasn't in the house. We had a separate house, on Lorelei Street. She had others who worked in the shop.

"I do know that the sum of my musical training, which was minimal, resulted from her beauty activities. There were some customers who couldn't pay. One was a piano teacher and as a result I ended up getting piano lessons. This was a few piano lessons just to pay off the bill. As you can imagine, I am not going to be challenging Rubenstein. That happened in Santa Barbara.

Venzor women, left to right: Jeanne, Natalia, Mary and Sarah.

"Then there was this other bill that was paid off with steel guitar lessons. So I learned a little bit of steel guitar.

"She didn't speak Spanish in the house to us. I do not know how to speak Spanish. My father could not speak Spanish and he was not about to allow me to learn to speak Spanish. If Jeanne got mad at him and said something to him in Spanish, he didn't want me to be the one who understood it.

"After the war, he found there were good prospects in California and he got into the aircraft industry and then he sent for me. I was raised by his parents. He sent for me and I came out and then became part of the family [with Jeanne.] I was the kid of the family. The others were older than me.

"I was definitely the kid, and they kind of dragged me around. They had to sort of babysit me. I was a teenager but I was young enough that I was not supposed to be left alone. I got to know a little bit of the culture. When the parents were gone, they'd have their friends over. They would play Spin the Bottle and I don't know what's going on. I saw couples going off to other rooms but I only had the vaguest idea what was going on."[195]

[Did you really see much of the Mexican side of the family?] "At our house in Bellflower, Sarah and Arnold would come once in a while and we'd have a barbecue, with the tortillas and the refried beans and the whole bit. Out on the back porch, Arnold would come out with his violin and we'd have a little mariachi. I loved that, and I still do love mariachi. I'm very much into Latin music; I took that away with me.

"Of course, I love all kinds of music. My father was a cantor. The one sort of bone that he threw to Spanish was that he and Jeanne had a song – a Spanish song – which I have not been able to locate, and I believe it was called 'El Borrachito' – The Drunkard. The Little Drunkard. He used to sing it all the time. Jeanne would play the piano and he would sing it. That seemed to me the most unifying thing in their relationship. That was all. Of course, he sung it very well, but I think that unless it was translated on the song sheet, he wouldn't really know what he was singing."

[Did he know that it was about drink?] "Yes. He definitely had to, because that was one of her problems. She used to be laid out on the couch. At night I'd go to bed and there she was, just snoring away. Sometimes she wasn't even lying down. She'd just be there in the chair, and she's gone – for the night. That was it.

"If you abused your body and you live a long time, it might be logical to think you could have lived a lot longer. I never saw Sarah drink. Jeanne talked about May, talked about her. Not a whole lot. I kind of remember the day that she informed me, 'You know, you've got a cousin…Ted Williams is your cousin.' I said, 'Really?' because I was a little bit of a baseball fan. I have to tell you, though, that I'm an Angels fan!

She told me about it one day and I said 'Really?' and she started telling me about the family, and the dysfunctionality of the family and May's problems with her relationship with Ted. This was fascinating. I was still kind of a kid, but having a father that had already been divorced three times, this wasn't totally new stuff for me, so I could identify a little bit.

[What do you think she meant when you talked about May's problems with Ted?] "It was so long ago, and this wasn't the most important thing in my life, and it's hazy in my memory but my impression was that there were problems in the family. Relationship problems. Some sort of conflict. They lived in San Diego, so it was not like we could go visiting. I know I never met Ted. I might have met May in Santa Barbara, but I can't remember. There were a lot of people there. I remember Bruno.

"I sort of got the feeling that May was so deep into her religion that that may have made her distant from her children. That's what the problem was that I referred to. This impressed me as a young person.

"I was raised ultra-Orthodox in Chicago. Typical big city type thing, because in the ghettoes of the big cities is where you get the concentration of the most fundamental orthodoxy. Typical Russian-type Jew. Straight Orthodox. The Germans tended to look down upon Yiddish, which was the bastardized language used in the Diaspora. The Germans thought this language was beneath them. But at the same temple, the same synagogue, you would have Germans and Russians.

"My wife is Catholic and we were married in the Unitarian church. It's sort of like where you sign peace treaties in a neutral territory.

"The yarmulke, that's really linked more with the Israelis. Most of the things that are worn are worn after the bar mitzvah. I was doing all the things that Orthodox do - the phylacteries and all of that, but when I came to California all of that was knocked out of me. It gradually got knocked out of me in the new environment because there was no support. My father was a cantor at a synagogue in Bellflower, but people in California were not very orthodox. He would only go on the high holidays.

"Jeanne was a Baptist. We would go to church. I think Jeanne was a little more loyal to her church than he was to his, in the sense of actually being religious, but I didn't see anything of the Salvation Army in Jeanne.

"My father was rather sensitive about the approval of his father in Chicago. His father, who had helped raise me, had conveyed to my father that he should not do anything to destroy my faith. The grandfather, being very orthodox, was very concerned.

[You had an adopted stepsister named Mary who was a Catholic, you had Jeanne who was Protestant and yourself who was Jewish. You had the whole Catholic/Jewish/Protestant thing in one household.] "Mary was probably the most religious in the house."

[It is interesting how Ted flew jet airplanes in Korea, and your father was in the aircraft industry, too] "I don't think I would have made all the connections that you are implying. My awareness of the world was not sufficient at the time; I'm trying to make up for it. My father didn't talk that way. It's funny. He didn't seem to be that proud of his work. It may be that, as a quality controller, he didn't feel that he was doing the building.

"I called her Jeanne. She was a good sort. Definitely. She had issues with my dad. Well, you can imagine my dad wasn't the easiest guy to get along with. With five marriages, he had an over-sized libido.

She was a real person. I call her 'real people.' I liked her. The one that followed, I sure didn't like. And number 3...she just seemed strange to me. I only saw her a little bit."

[Did you keep in touch with Jeanne after they divorced?] "A little bit. Not much. It sort of petered out. I was so busy with my own work."

[Did Jeanne have any pictures of Ted Williams up on her wall, for instance?] "No. There may have been a photograph in an album, but nothing on the wall. There weren't family pictures displayed on the wall. There wasn't much of that in our family at all. It didn't come up a lot. What would be the basis? What would be the context? Jeanne and Sooky weren't excited about baseball. They didn't seem to have any interest in baseball. I was the one who listened to the radio and listened to the ballgames. I was a Cubs and White Sox fan. I would listen to these re-creations of games. That was my interest in baseball, very vicarious. I seemed to be the only family member that was interested in baseball at all. When I heard that I was somehow related to Ted, that was of interest to me. But the baseball part of it wasn't of interest to anybody. Sure I'd heard of him! Oh, sure! You knew about him or you were an idiot."[196]

Judaism was a new element in the family. "We had a very unusual household. Abby and I did not even know about the Jewish religion, until Howard moved in with us. Then he thought that I was just too nosy and asked too many questions regarding his religion. But I just wanted to know more, in the meantime I have read more on that subject."[197]

Jeanne's alcoholism presented some serious problems, and by the time she personally reformed, it was apparently too late to spare her children the curse. Manuel remembers, "Jennie was drunk every time we visited and Pop always had a bottle of whiskey to honor the occasion. My sister and I often sat at Aunt Jeanie's beauty shop while Sarah got her hair done and that was a long wasted evening for us kids, especially with Jean and Pop drunk!"[198]

"Natalia Venzor was the quiet hero and leader of the family. No one dare abuse me or my sister in her sight, but when she died the protection was gone and the uncles and aunts were very abusive to us. Saul was the worst, he lived to be 60 years old but looked like 90 when he died. I hated him because he made my young life very unhappy and miserable just like Bruno. Paul was rude when he was drunk and if he didn't drink he kept to himself. Aunt Jean or Jenny as Ted called her, was an out and out drunk. She could really put the booze away and had no shame. Her two kids hated her and how she acted! Abby had no contact with her mother at all and Joseph is in a rest home where he is an alcoholic and is suffering from brain damage which he got while in a fight. He nearly died, but he is still alive and has no idea who he is or where he is at. A sad situation and life. His kids are heavy drug addicts, heroin and cocaine. A sad ending. Aunt Jean did clean up her life, but the impression she put in my mind has never changed."[199]

A sad situation, for sure. One interesting reward for me in doing my research into the Venzor family has been the ability to prompt a few reunions. Howard Winet and Mary Redding had not been in touch with each other for nearly half a century. When I interviewed Howard in November 2002, I learned that he hadn't been in contact with Mary for many years. Having previously interviewed Mary two and a half years earlier, I gave them each the other's e-mail addresses. In the summer of 2003, Howard and his wife Carol took a trip from Los Angeles and met Mary again in person. He dropped me this note later in the year: "I'd like to thank you most deeply for getting Mary and me together after 48 years. Carol and I drove to Laurel, Montana last summer and visited with her and her husband Bob. The conversations were nonstop, and tears often blurred sight. I learned much that was hidden from me in the 50s and uncovered much I had hidden from myself since."[200] There were other reunions as well, in the event at the San Diego Hall of Champions.

Daniel Arthur Williams, July 20, 1920 - March 28, 1960

Having learned something about each of Ted's maternal uncles and aunts, let's try to learn more about his brother Danny, and just a bit about Danny's children.

As indicated above, Danny Williams has come down to us in the accounts as a one-dimensional, even distasteful character – a troublemaker who was a source of anguish and bother to his big brother Ted, and a trial to his mother as well.

Is this all Danny Williams was?

Reading about Ted's younger brother Danny, one gets the impression that he was a bad egg, a ne'er-do-well, or worse. Ed Linn introduced readers to Danny Williams very succinctly as "a juvenile delinquent, a small-time thief, a jailbird, a bum."[201]

A chapter later, we're told, "Danny ran with the bad kids. He stole. He packed a gun. He was thrown out of five or six schools." We're told that Ted brought home his first car, a brand-new 1938 Buick, and he soon found the car up on cement blocks. "Danny had stripped all the tires and sold them." After the 1941 season, Ted paid for the renovation of May Williams' home on Utah Street, but "Danny promptly backed a truck up to the house, moved out all the new furniture, including a washing machine and a sewing machine, and sold it." Linn tells us that May finally quit trying to get Danny out of trouble with the authorities and "had him arrested. He spent some time in San Quentin -- not that it seemed to do any good."[202]

The San Diego Police Department supposedly termed Danny "the city's most incorrigible youth" and someone the United States Army once arrested as a deserter.[203] There are stories upon stories of Danny's escapades and scrapes with the law. He comes across as someone with no redeeming qualities whatsoever. A surly kid who stewed in spiteful envy of his talented older brother, Ted Williams, who found fame and fortune and left his less-gifted younger brother in a dark shadow. It's a vivid yet tragic portrait; Danny Williams comes across as a pretty one-dimensional character, someone we could all enjoy kicking around.

Was this a fair portrayal? Was he really as uni-dimensional as we've been led to believe? Later in Linn's book, he grants that Danny "straightened himself out...found work as a contract painter and interior decorator. He had married, he had a couple of kids, and he had reconciled with his older brother."[204]

Ted himself had relatively little to say about his kid brother. What he did write was more sympathetic than accusatory. Ted faults his mother and father for Danny turning out differently. Ted felt he himself was very lucky to have families like the Cassies and men like Rod Luscomb encouraging him, and welcoming him into their homes. The lack of a close-knit family home, though, hurt Danny. "I know Danny suffered because of it," he wrote. "I have to think poor Danny had a tormented life. He wasn't an athlete. He threw an orange at somebody one time and just throwing the orange broke his arm. They found out he had leukemia in the bone marrow and with any kind of violent movement, *snap*, a bone would go. Danny was always more interested in cars and other things, the kind of guy who wanted a motorcycle and never got it. He hung out with an altogether different bunch, and I suppose a lot of people thought he was surly and mean, but I have to think he was just terribly tormented.

"I know he was a thorn in my mother's side, always getting into scrapes. Nothing really serious, but one jam after another – piling up traffic tickets, maybe stealing a bicycle, or owing money on a truck and trying to clear out without paying. Rod Luscomb took a loaded revolver away from him one time."[205]

Ted recognized that "some guys have absolutely no respect for authority, and Danny was one of them." He then proceeded to indicate sympathy for Danny. "There wasn't the closeness between us there should have been. I regret that. After I left for pro ball, I never saw much of him. He used to use my name for things, and I'd have to bail him out, which was unpleasant for both of us. My being in the public eye probably made it tougher for him. He never had too many advantages. He never had the outlets for expression I did. His life was just an existence. He died tough. I got his little pistol. I always thought he would shoot himself because he suffered so much."[206]

Danny died at age 39. He's gone down in history with a bad rap. Surely, it didn't come from nowhere, and much of it was well-deserved, but it can't have been easy living a sometimes sickly life in the shadow of a great athlete, feeling short-changed by life. Who among us would find that a burden we could handle with equanimity?

There really are some fascinating stories about Danny's run-ins with the law, or his running away from trouble. Right near the house, at the University Heights (North Park) playground, there is a large water tower. Any young boy would be intrigued with the possibilities. Danny decided to climb the tower. "Danny was so different from Ted," explained Sarah Diaz. "Danny felt very inferior. He wanted to play ball; he couldn't. He wanted to do what Ted could do; he couldn't. But to attract attention, he did a lot of very odd things. Close to his home on Utah Street, 4121 Utah Street, that's where the park was where Ted used to practice, right there by the school. There was a big water tank, way up on stilts, wooden, and Danny climbed way up the top of that tower and then he couldn't get down. So somebody had to go and look for May. She was out selling *War Cry*s. When they found her, they told her and so she had to come home. She had to call the fire department to get him down. But he wasn't anything like Ted. He was a little scoundrel. He used to do the darndest things just to attract attention, because

Young Danny Williams in front of 4121 Utah Street.

Ted was getting all the fame and doing all the good things that he couldn't do."[207]

The way Manuel tells it, it wasn't just that he couldn't get down – he didn't want to come down! "'Tell them to get the cops! I ain't coming down until they get the cops! Bring the fire department, too!' Attention. He wanted attention. He caused a scene."[208]

That was a time he wanted the cops to come. There were times he was trying to flee them. One of his cousins, Teresa Cordero Contreras, remembers one of those times, around 1936. Danny turned 16 that year. "He was a crazy guy. He tried to sell anything. One time when I was about 7 or 8, my mother sent me up there to help Aunt May because Ted had started playing for the Padres. He was going to remodel her kitchen, make it bigger. My mom sent me up there to help. Danny was there all the time. He was a character. We were going to go to the store and he had an old car. My Uncle Samuel, he was a jail inspector and I guess Danny figured he could just do anything he wanted to. We went to the store and then all of a sudden he went past a stop sign. Then here's a cop, right behind him. We raced through San Diego in his old Model A, you know, without the hood – you know, how they used to strip them. We went through all the streets and alleys, and then all of a sudden we went into somebody's garage, and the police went by! I was so scared, and my Aunt May was just furious. She just couldn't get over how dumb he was to do such a thing. I guess he figured his dad could fix it up. I don't know, I was only 7."[209]

Danny wasn't the only family figure who was a little wild. Teresa's sister Madeline Cordero was quite a character herself. "My fighting Aunt Madeline," Manuel Herrera called her. Sarah Diaz had told Manny, "Your Aunt Madeline is one tough gal. She has fighting ability and could beat any girl around, not to mention her brothers…I got my first taste of her capabilities when I was walking my brother Paul back to his house on the East Side. There were Mexican bars on Haley Street and a fight was part of the evening. We were talking and heading east to his house when we passed the El Poche. Suddenly a short Mexican national was flying out the entrance, and soon there was another, flying by the neck and seat of his pants. It was my Aunt Madeline tossing this guy out of the bar. She was pissed, to put it mildly. 'Don't you Mexicans know how to treat a lady?' Hell, them guys were running down the street the minute they could get up off the ground. My fighting Aunt Madeline then looked right at my brother and me as we were laughing and she said, 'What are you doing here? Get your asses home!' as she returned to the bar.

"The next fight was across from my friend's restaurant. I was at Joe's Cafe enjoying a meal and five cop cars pulled up and they headed into Sammy's Bar and Grill across the street. The cops had my cousin Sooky handcuffed in the police car. He was just trying to help Aunt Madeline whip ole Big Betty. Sooky wasn't really needed for support; Aunt Madeline had Big Betty against the wall and was throwing body shots into Betty. I sure was happy to know that my aunt had the situation well under control. Madeline knocked off the toughest gal in town with no trouble; she was the champ of Santa Barbara. The cops finally stopped the fight and cuffed both gals and hauled them off to jail. I later heard she got six months. Since she had plenty of time and could knit very well, she knitted Captain Sheriff Ross a sweater and got off three months early for good behavior. Sheriff Ross was a friend of the family and gave her a break, but he did like the sweater."[210] Sooky Moreno "should have been an actor, playing a Pachuco or a tough Mexican James Dean, because he was a real character and loved attention. He drove a Harley hog and had the road rash to prove it. I liked him, but he was always in and out of jail."[211]

When Madeline and Danny teamed up, well, it was something special. "Old Danny liked to get her riled up and that was something he could easily do. Danny and Madeline went down to a local bar to have a few beers. As the story goes, Danny began to get Madeline going, [taunting her, saying that] she couldn't fight. Aunt Madeline told Danny she could and made a wager with him that she could take on anyone in the bar. Just about that time, two cops walked in, and Danny suggested to Madeline that she take on those cops. Well, Aunt Madeline was stirred up and she was out to prove her worth, so she walked up to the first cop and dropped him like a sack of potatoes. Then the next cop went down like struck lightning. My aunt made it to the door and ran out of the place like a track star!

"Danny sat on his bar stool and laughed his butt off as Madeline ran out of the bar. The guys at the bar wanted to know who was that lady, but Danny wouldn't give out any clues. Danny had the ability to get Madeline worked up, and he enjoyed the results as well! I think the word that describes Danny is 'antagonize.' He loved to taunt people. Danny had the ability to get anyone antagonized and Ted was no exception. Teddy paid many a bill that Danny charged, up in Santa Barbara. The word was, 'Ted is my brother, I'm Danny Williams and Ted will pay this bill.' I heard it was done many a time." Manuel added: "You must realize Aunt Madeline was raised with some tough brothers and fought often. She was built like a Mack truck and learned to use her mitts at a young age. Her hands were very big like mine, extra large, and she drove a truck at an early age. My grandfather owned a trucking business and she loaded and hauled hay just like her brothers. She could trade punches with the best in town. The Cordero family liked Danny much more than Teddy. Ted was serious, but Danny was out for a good time."[212]

The police got their hands on Danny more than a few times, though. Even as young as the age of 12, Danny spent considerable time at the Anthony

The water tower at the North Park playground.

Home, located on Texas Street. It was a home for juveniles under 16. "He used to spend half his time down there," said Joe Villarino.[213] Joe told Tom Larwin that he knows Danny was caught at least once selling stolen tires. When he'd hocked all his mom's furniture in early 1942, he was 21 and he was reportedly arrested, but in the end May refused to sign a complaint. "Employing the technicality that with all the furniture gone from the Williams' home it therefore became uninhabitable, the cops jailed Danny as a vagrant. The latter pleaded guilty, got the top misdemeanor rap – 180 days and a $500 fine – but sentence was suspended when Danny agreed to leave town."[214] When he left town, it may have been to join the Army. He enlisted on February 16, 1942.

Madeline Cordero Flores.

If the police once termed Danny "the city's most incorrigible youth," it was a characterization picked up by others as well. Leonard Bell was a teammate of Ted's at Hoover High. He later became Fire Chief for the City of San Diego. Bell told about a time he'd come across Danny on the roadside. "Danny Williams was kind of incorrigible. He was hitchhiking down Pershing Drive. So I picked him up and said, 'Where you going, Danny?' He said, 'I'm supposed to be in court, but the hell with it; I'm just going to ignore them.' I think he was one of the reasons Ted never came back to San Diego off season."[215]

Danny was born on July 20, 1920 in San Diego and he died March 28, 1960 at Mercy Hospital in San Diego, and is buried at Memorial Gardens in San Diego. He was living at 4121 Utah Street at the time of his death, but had entered the hospital seven days before his final passing. He was listed in his obituary as a decorator and painter, but it was noted that he had been disabled for 2 1/2 years. The hospital reported that the cause of death was a malignancy of the bone marrow.

He left a widow, the former Betty Jean Klein, and three sons. Two sons, Sam and Ted, were referred to in passing in one or two of the books about Ted Williams. It turns out there was also a son by an earlier marriage, Danny Jr., who had never been mentioned in other writings.

I knew Danny had two sons, Ted and Sam. As indicated above, I first met them at the Fenway Park remembrance ceremony for Ted Williams in July 2002. I've kept in close touch with Ted ever since, with a visit to his house in Oakland and with several hundred e-mails back and forth. Ted and his wife Sue have a young son Noah, who's off to a pretty good start in baseball himself at the age of 11. Like his grandfather, Ted also is an accomplished photographer. He has the largest collection of Venzor family photographs and papers I've come across – sadly, most of it fits in one box. Ted is also a talented graphic artist and is the designer of two books I wrote or edited: *The Kid: Ted Williams in San Diego and Ted Williams at War.* Sam inspired me to write *521: The Story of Ted Williams' Home Runs* and wrote the foreword to the book.

Danny's son Samuel Stuart Williams was born in San Diego on May 7, 1950. John Theodore Williams was born in Fort Worth, Texas on October 21, 1951. John Theodore was always called "Ted" – the "John" came from his maternal grandfather, John Earl Calvin Klein (who was himself known as Earl – not Calvin Klein!) Earl was a Chevrolet mechanic who had his own garage, but the family was a very poor one and had seen rough times.

Danny's son Ted told me, "The Kleins are from Germany. They were just German; they weren't Jewish. They came from Pennsylvania, I believe, in 1870 to Texas. They came from Pennsylvania. My grandfather never had anything. My mother said that during the Depression they lived under a bridge in old abandoned cars. Basically it was flour and water gravy.

"But her aunt had farmed. They had a lot of fresh produce and vegetables, although my mother hated it. I don't know why. When we were kids, she always loved canned peaches, canned corn. Everything was canned because she never had that. She loved canned stuff. Then she'd boil it for about an hour or so (laughs.) She never made a fresh vegetable. Maybe asparagus.

"Her famous story was that here they were living under the bridge in these car bodies, and my grandfather just had it one time. So he said, 'I can't stand seeing my kids hungry any more' and he went and stole a cow, from his sister, my mom's aunt, who had this farm. He slaughtered it to feed them. She arrested him and threw him in jail. Ever since, they were bitter enemies."[216]

EVENING TRIBUNE
SAN DIEGO, CALIFORNIA
Tuesday, May 29, 1968 B-23

D. A. Williams, 39, Kin of Ted, Dies

DANIEL WILLIAMS
Native San Diegan

Jesse N. Douglas

Danny's wife Jean Klein lost a brother in World War II. Vance Klein, 19, was killed in the Mediterranean theater in 1943.

What about this other son, Danny's first-born? Neither Sam nor Ted remembered ever meeting him, but they'd heard about him, and Ted had a sympathy card in with some old photographs May Williams had saved, signed "Mr. and Mrs. Daniel Williams Jr." Ted wrote me in August, 2002: "So maybe the other son had the same name?" It had never been a secret. "We knew about it, but we never knew where he was or who he was or how to contact him."[217]

It intrigued me that Ted and Sam might have a half-brother out there, but they didn't know if he were living or deceased. They had had no contact. As late as December, 2002, they weren't really sure if there was still a Danny Jr. out there. I decided to try to find out.

If he were a true "junior," then his name would be Daniel Arthur Williams, Jr. There were hundreds upon hundreds of listings for Daniel Williams in the state of California, and many telephone listings don't permit searches by middle name. There was, though, a site www.ussearch.com, which does accept middle names to help narrow searches of their data bases. They also permit you to search by approximate age. Entering "Daniel A. Williams," I came up with 61 names in California. Only one seemed to be around the right age – a 63-year-old man living in Arcadia, California. He didn't have a listed telephone. The only way to find his address was to pay U.S. Search. com a fee of $9.95 (it's how they make their money). I did, and received an address (but no phone number) by return mail. I promptly mailed off a letter introducing myself and explaining that I was researching Ted Williams and his brother Danny, and if this were one of Danny's sons, could he please write back and let me know if I could speak with him? I heard nothing.

After a couple of months, when Ted and I were talking, I told him I'd written but had no response, and then suggested that Ted write him. I hunted up where I had the address, and sent it to Ted. He wrote and, not too long afterward, heard back. First contact was made on January 7, 2003. "Well, I talked to him," Ted e-mailed me. "[He] seemed really glad to hear from me, no hard feelings, in fact didn't know Danny much at all." Danny Jr. did exist. He'd come to his father's funeral in 1960, but of course Ted was only 8 years old and he'd just lost his father and his mother was distraught, and it wasn't a memory that took. Danny Jr. was alive and living in southern California. Interestingly, he, too, had become a graphic designer.

In March 2003, Dan and Ted first really met, at the daylong event honoring Ted Williams at the San Diego Hall of Champions. This event offered the opportunity for the two half-brothers to meet, really for the first time. When Ted met Dan and his wife Jan outside the doors of the Hall of Champions before the day's program began, it was the reunion of two brothers who had effectively never met. Their father, Danny, had met Helen Hansen at San Diego High. It was a very short-lived marriage, but in some ways an intense one. "He didn't leave. She divorced him," Dan told me, after informing me that he had been born in 1940, on May 4. His father stuck around for three

years, but he was raised by his mother and grandmother. Dan's wife Jan (they were married in 1971) told me that she'd heard that Helen had taken out a restrain-

Danny Williams with his boys from his second marriage, Sam and Ted, in Chicago about 1953.

ing order against Danny. "I don't know what that was all about. He was very young."[218]

Danny had joined the army early in 1942, but it seems that he found it very difficult to be away from his wife and young son. So he'd take off and go see them. With or without permission. "My mother told me Danny was dishonorably discharged from the Army for constantly going AWOL to go see his son."[219]

Later in 2003, Ted filed a request for information with the Army, but was only able to learn the dates of Daniel Williams' service, February 16, 1942 to August 18, 1943, that he had held the rank of private, and that his separation from the Army was with an "other than honorable discharge."

There was a war going on, and a soldier who would show little respect for rules and regulations was not going to be a productive soldier. Sarah Diaz told Manuel that the MPs had thrown Pvt. Williams in the brig but he'd broken the toilets and flooded the facility, and escaped while they were trying to deal with the damage. The MPs showed up at 1008 Chino Street, hot on his trail, but he wasn't hiding there.[220] They may have been glad to see the last of him.

By August 1943, too, the marriage had broken up. Helen Hansen found a place in public housing, and eventually remarried. Dan Jr. does recall his dad visiting one time and bringing an electric train. What Danny Williams did for the next few years is unclear. Sometime around 1947, though, he met Betty Jean Klein, when she was 15. He was 10 or more years older. Perhaps she couldn't wait to escape the poverty in Fort Worth, where she was raised with nine brothers and sisters.

Neither Ted nor Sam really know the story, and whenever they've asked one of their aunts in Texas, they get nowhere. It's a taboo subject. No one wants to talk about Danny. "One of the things I find is that when you ask questions about Danny, a lot of the time people clam up."[221] There were appar-

Earl Klein with a couple of his buckaroo
grandsons, Texas.

ently a couple of miscarriages, but Sam was born in 1950, three months prematurely.

Danny and Jean married and began to raise a family. With two children and a pretty young wife, Danny may have begun to settle down some. That didn't mean that life became easy. He worked, and worked hard, as did Jean. "When we were in Chicago," Ted told me, "both he and my mom worked. We would go to school and when we came from school we would stay with a neighbor that lived in the apartment below...some retired people...until they got home. She was working in a restaurant -- a fairly famous restaurant in Chicago. She was a waitress."

Danny had talents and found pleasures in working with his talents. "He liked painting. I think he was artistic. When we were in Chicago, he painted this huge mural of the city of Chicago across the living room wall. I'm sure the building hated him for it, but he was just obsessed. He would do that kind of stuff. It was not easy. It was huge. He did a few paintings on canvas. My brother has one, of a bullfighter. I don't know if he was a great artist, but it excited him. He liked doing it. It was probably that busy-ness, too. He needed to do something all the time. He puttered with his truck. You saw that picture. That was a truck he bought. He had a red one that was just like that, that I think he bought in Chicago that we drove to Chicago – or that he drove to Chicago; we took the train. But it was not that long after that it disappeared; I think it got repossessed. So he got that used one. In that picture he was in the process of fixing it up. He was painting the inside with a brush. He spent all his time doing that kind of stuff, fixing up cars. He loved his car.

"I remember him building stuff. Making shelves. He was always doing that kind of stuff. Even in Chicago, he made Sam and I each these kind of wall-hanging things – panels that we could hang our clothes on, they had little drawers. They were complicated little things. He made us each one so we could put our stuff away in our bedroom. He framed pictures. He had pictures of the jets Ted used to fly. We had those around on the walls. He liked to read. He had a fair number of books. He liked picture books."

"We bounced around a lot for some reason. I don't know why. Well, again, I think Danny was probably dodging his bills. Texas for a while. And Chicago. San Diego. And back. And back, and back. That was kind of our triangle."[222]

Danny and Jean liked to go out when they could, to dinner and dancing. "They would like to go out at night and sometimes they would just leave us alone at night and just go out. We'd cause lots of trouble when they were gone. [laughs] It's a wonder we didn't die, the things we did. We didn't go out, but one time they left us alone in that apartment building. We were on the sixth floor. We were playing...there was a little bathroom, and we were playing and we got in there and somehow the doorknob came apart and fell on the floor, so we couldn't get out the door. We were locked in the bathroom. We realized we could climb out the window and crawl along the ledge that was right out the window to get to the next window and hop back into the living room, which we did. And then since we had no supervision and no controls, we realized, hey, I guess that ledge goes all the way around the building! So we crawled all the way around the building. On the sixth floor. On this little concrete ledge.

"Another night they went out at night and we were left at home. They stayed out pretty late and we were doing something and we spilled some water on the kitchen floor, on the linoleum. We realized

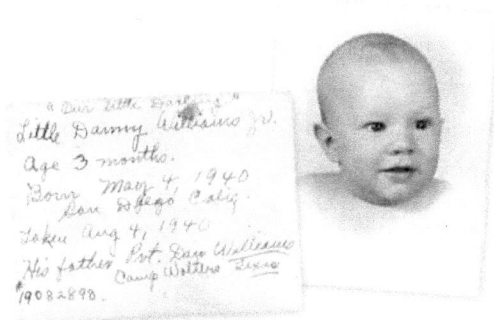

A photograph of Dan Jr. carried by his father, Danny Williams when he was in the army.

that this made a great slip and slide, so then we just started getting buckets of water and poured it on the floor and we played that for a long time. I remember that as one of the most fun times we ever had! My brother says we got beat pretty bad. It sure was fun. I'm not surprised if people below didn't come up because we probably flooded their place, too. Sam and I talked about that when we were in Boston. That was really fun."[223]

All in all, though, it seemed like Danny was trying to be a decent family man. He'd often take little Ted with him when he went on jobs. He'd paint some big apartment buildings in Chicago, painting interiors all day long, all by himself. He'd tell Ted not to bother him, and Ted would wander off and explore the building. The only fun part of it, though, was when they went to lunch together. "We usually went to lunch in a bar, so he could have a beer. I thought it was really fun to sit at the counter of the bar with everyone drinking."[224]

Danny never drank much, maybe one beer at lunch. Neither Danny or Jean were drinkers. It's very refreshing to hear Ted and Sam talk about life when they were young children, because it leaves us with a picture of Danny Williams as someone who was complex and human, not simply the image we've been given of someone "incorrigible" and maybe even evil.

Danny did eventually move the family back to San Diego to stay. They moved in with May Williams, and it was a nice time for the kids, innocent as they were of much that went on around them. "San Diego was actually a wonderful time. The weather was beautiful. We were out all the time. It was a time when kids just ran. We rode our bikes clear to Balboa Park, however far that was. We were at the playground all the time. There were all kinds of kids on the street. My best friend was across the street. We were just always out playing. We went to school. We played. We might clean up the yard a little bit sometimes, but we didn't have a lot of responsibilities."[225]

There could have even been another ballplayer in the family. Sam Williams played Little League in San Diego for a year or two. Outfield. His eyes were never good. "I think my biggest problem was concentration, though," he laughs. University Heights (North Park) was "a wonderful playground. It was all dirt when we were kids. We used to play there. That's all we did. Played baseball. It was so close and the weather was so good. The fence sure seemed a long way away." Sam played ball more than his younger brother Ted. "One of the things that probably turned him off to sports was how competitive I was. I don't have any doubt that I probably would have tried to pursue baseball if my eyes were better. It was a liability."[226]

Moving back to Utah Street placed Danny and family back in his childhood home, and with his mother May. Both Ted and Danny were concerned about their mother, and – regardless of all the vitriol that Manuel noticed – the two brothers did have a relationship. Danny found May's place a little chaotic. She may have been turning a bit senile. He took some photographs of the back yard to send brother Ted, to provide Ted a sense of how things were.

May was apparently a packrat. She kept everything. "When we moved into her house, she had every room stacked with stuff almost to the ceiling, and she just had little trails to get through the rooms. Newspapers...she saved everything on Ted Williams, and I'm sorry we lost it all, because she used to have these huge scrapbooks of everything. But she would also just save every daily paper. She was not very discriminating. Then, unfortunately, to make room for all the unimportant stuff she was saving in the house, all the Ted Williams stuff she put out in the garage where the roof was leaking. It was just all destroyed by water. I just remember boxes and boxes. Books and...I don't know. Maybe old clothes. Even in the living room. The dining room. She had moved out all the furniture. I think towards the end of her life she was going a little senile and maybe some [little] things became equally important with other things that she did."[227]

Danny Williams painting the inside of his truck with a brush, in the driveway at 4121 Utah Street, about 1958.

165

She also had the habit of writing thoughts down, even just the briefest of little notes to herself, like how much she loved her precious boys or moments of prayer, such as "Oh! Dear Lord, stand by me." She would write out their birth dates (she always wrote August 30 for Ted's), sometimes many times on many pieces of paper. Her grandson Ted has saved some of the papers and we can sense that her writing was what today we would call obsessive-compulsive. You'd find her writings on everything, Ted told me. "You'd find it on everything. Scraps of paper, the margins of magazine, receipts, on the edges of newspapers. It was on everything. "228

The writing was in English. When Ted was less than two years old, however, at the time of the 1920 census, May Williams told the census taker that her native language was Spanish. As we've seen, May's mother – who Ted knew – always spoke in Spanish.

May always called her sons "Precious." Ted never recalls her uttering a negative word about either child. "From her writings, I can see they were equally precious to her. That's one thing about the Venzor family that I felt, even about going to see Sarah and stuff – even though Ted was this superstar, they didn't distinguish between family members. They all loved each other equally....I never felt like I was secondary because I was Danny's kid and not Ted's. I felt very loved and wanted and desired and appreciated by any family members that I came across."229

Ted remembers that Danny was far from uniformly negative or hostile toward his brother. Danny urged his kids to get into sports, as a good way to make a living. Young Ted may have been shielded a bit – in which case we need to give his father credit for that – but he was able to tell me in 2002, "I don't

MY EXPERIENCE IS YOUR PROTECTION

Dan Williams
PAINTING AND DECORATING
CONTRACTOR

4121 UTAH STREET
SAN DIEGO, CALIF.

PHONE R 6929

Danny's business card, after he returned to San Diego and his mother's home, suffering from leukemia.

recall him ever saying anything negative about Ted. He was very proud of him. He was very...there was love there. I never had the feeling [that he tried to badmouth Ted]. He loved to tell stories about Ted. He loved to say things that Ted had said. Little comments, biting comments. He had photographs of the jets Ted flew. He was proud of that stuff. I have so many pictures of Bobby-Jo because he'd send them to May and he'd send them to Danny. [Danny] liked Ted. I don't think there was any negative feeling. He might have been embarrassed by some of his behavior, some of his taking advantage of Ted – if he had those feelings, but I don't know if that was true."

He knew that Danny was angry, that he was upset, that he felt slighted in life, that maybe he somehow was even owed something. Certainly some of that came from his brother being so successful, and him not. "I think that was the source of Danny's anger. I think that was more his personal tribulation, though, than something he attributed as Ted's fault. He spoke about him [Ted] very lovingly. He was proud of him, not just his accomplishments but as a brother, as family, as a companion."[230]

At the same time, the superstar ballplayer wasn't that adept at relationships. Ted didn't come home all that often, and sometimes it probably just seemed easier to him to throw money at a problem than to grapple with it personally. Ted the nephew knew that there were times that Danny abused the relationship and Ted the brother had to bail him out. It was a subject of some sensitivity. All in all, though, matters were just not as "black and white" as they have been portrayed in print.

It's not as though Danny ever became angelic. He carried a pistol – which he may have acquired when doing some non-union work in Chicago. Manuel Herrera said there was one time that May didn't want to get into the car with her son one time in Santa Barbara. "He was trying to get May in the Packard Clipper he owned and she was talking too long, so old Danny had enough of that and fired off a round. He carried a pistol, a .32 special and fired it at the hill where we lived when Aunt May wouldn't get into the car. I was there when he pulled the trigger on his .32 stubbie, then he looked at me and

Nephews Ted, left, and Sam Williams, right, playing baseball for the North Park Little League, about 1959.

laughed. My poor Aunt May thought Danny was going to kill her and she pleaded, 'Danny, don't shoot me. I'll get in the car, just don't shoot.' I can hear her saying that right now."[231]

When Danny got sick with cancer, things got worse. It's hard to judge another person, unless you have been in that person's shoes. Facing death -- and leukemia almost inevitably let to death in the late 1950s – it is hard to judge the behavior of another. We can try to understand. Here was Ted Williams, on the one hand. Ted had enjoyed a tremendously successful career, winning batting titles in 1957 and 1958. He was the highest paid player in baseball. He'd also earned additional glory as a decorated fighter pilot in Korea. And here was Danny Williams, on the other hand, struggling to get by financially, laboring hard at work, and he gets hit with cancer of the bone marrow. There's no question he still had the short end of the stick, and his grip was weakening.

He knew he was dying, and he knew that one of the only hopes he had was to get the best medical treatment available. Who paid for that treatment? His super-successful big brother. All the old envy and jealousy resurfaced. No one likes to be fully dependent on another, and yet here was Danny living back at 4121 Utah Street with an aging mother, dependent on Ted to cover the bills (and the air ambulance flights to Salt Lake City for treatment by the leading specialist of the day). He was dependent on Jean for the morphine injections that addressed his pain. Near the end, with Danny wasting away, Jean even had to light his cigarettes for him. Is it any wonder that the bitterness and spite resurfaced? It had probably never been that deeply buried, in any event.

"He looked frail, like a Jewish prisoner of war," remembered Manuel Herrera.[232] Danny was of different stature than Ted. A temporary drivers license issued in San Diego on 9/23/59 has him listed as 5'11" and 140 pounds. He'd already lost considerable weight by that time, but by no means did he have the 6' 4" frame of his famous brother. But he was angry, and he had a hateful streak. Danny visited Santa Barbara at one time when Manuel was in eighth or ninth grade. "He was awfully ill at the time. He sat right down next to me while I was doing my homework and for four days, he didn't have a good thing to say about his brother. It broke my heart. It confused me as a young kid. I have never met a person who hated his brother more than Danny Williams. He didn't have one good word about his brother!"[233]

Ted had him brought to see Dr. Winthrop at St. Mary's in Salt Lake City and to the Mayo Clinic in Rochester, Minnesota, even to a cancer hospital in Tijuana. "He told me, 'I know my brother's paying for whatever. I hope it cost him a bundle. I'll take him for every cent he's got.' I said, 'Danny, he's trying to help.' He said, 'I don't give a damn,' and he went on and on. I just shut down."[234]

Manuel understood, though. "I could see that he was really a good guy but he was trying to get acceptance and attention. He knew he was dying and his family would be without him. He laughed things off, but I could see that he was hurting inside."[235]

There are other perspectives, though. It's possible that Danny was talking tough to Manuel, more or less for what we might call "public consumption." In private, things may have been different. Danny's son Ted said, "I'm sure Danny gave him a lot of grief, but I saw Ted being very warm and compassionate to Danny. He literally did everything he could, and it was mostly money but he cared immensely in his own way, too. I remember Danny telling us over and over when we were kids, 'Don't bother your uncle. He hates being bothered, and whatever you do, don't ask him for any money."[236] Through it all, though, Ted was taking financial care of his mother, and his brother, and his brother's family.

"It was really hard for my mom, loving him, knowing she was losing him, taking care of him, worrying about him, us, money, taking his abuse, which turned verbal when he could no longer be physical. He was literally bedridden the last year or so, she had to do everything for him, feed him, wash him, give him morphine injections, light his cigarettes. She never complained."[237]

In the end, Danny found peace at last. He left this world with at least one gesture of good will, apologizing to Jean for all she'd had to go through. "She told me once that when he died, he told her he was sorry for being so mean."[238]

How is Danny remembered now? A bit of an enigma, says his son Ted. He had some demons. Maybe he got some of those from his father Samuel. But he worked hard. He tried, in his own way. And he suffered. In the end, one can feel for him, the burdens he bore.

Sadly, we lost Ted on August 19, 2014.

OTHER FAMILY MEMBERS

There are, of course, other Venzors out there. Not to mention Hernandezes, Rubios and others. I called a few. In January 2003, I spoke to Lionel Venzor of El Paso. He wasn't sure of his background, but knew that his mother came from the Rubio side of the family. His grandmother was a Carbajal, and Lionel said he was named after his Uncle Lionel Carbajal of Santa Barbara. Both sides of the family came from Chihuahua. He'd once tried to trace down Venzors in Madrid and Sevilla, but with no luck. He thinks the Venzors were connected to the Morga family in some fashion. He'd never heard of any Ted Williams connection, though. If a researcher had enough time, there are certainly deeper family connections that could be explored.

I felt good that I was able to help bring Ted Williams and Dan Williams, Jr. together. At the same SABR/Hall of Champions event, Dan also met Karma Barber, who had grown up with Ted and Sam, after Danny's widow had married Dave Barber. All told, the event in San Diego drew at least 33 family members together for the day of discussion about their Hall of Fame relative (actually, Ted Williams is in 10 Halls of Fame, at last count.) For many, it was the first time they had ever met others in the family. As indicated above, some of the reunions still continue, as Howard Winet drove to Montana to meet Mary Redding. There will no doubt be others in the days to come.

And I do hope, someday, to learn more of significance about Ted's father's side of the family – maybe from that elusive niece or nephew who may or may not have ever been born.

There has been some other baseball played in the family as well.

OTHER FAMILY MEMBERS WHO PLAYED BASEBALL

Aside from Ted Williams and some of the *tios* Venzor, there have been a few other family members who have played baseball. Of course, the one who received the most attention in recent years was Ted's own son, John-Henry Williams. John-Henry tried out for the college team at Bates College, but didn't make the first cut. Had he ever made the majors, however, he would by no means have been the first ballplayer who'd been cut by his college team. John-Henry transferred to the University of Maine at Orono, and showed some initial interest but never truly tried out for the team. Born in 1968, John-Henry's first serious attempt at baseball came in 2002 when he was 33 years old; he signed with the Gulf Coast Red Sox in late June. The club was an affiliate of the Boston Red Sox and most observers assumed that the only reason John-Henry was signed was out of respect for his father, the greatest Red Sox player of all time. He never did get a hit for the Gold Coast team and, in just the second game he played, John-Henry broke a rib chasing a foul ball that fell in the seats. Give him credit for effort. Eight days later, Ted Williams died.

Whatever others might say, Ted himself was proud of his son and glad that he decided to take a shot at baseball. Even in the last weeks of Ted's life, a friend of John-Henry's reported that Ted "was lying in his bed talking to a member of his nursing staff. He had a big Ted Williams smile on his face. The nurse asked him what he was smiling about. Ted told the nurse, ``You know I'm really proud of John Henry (sic) playing pro baseball. I never pushed him toward it, but I'm real glad he's doing it now."[239]

The following year, John-Henry enlisted the help of a full-time hitting instructor and worked out with expensive equipment. Ted's son gave it all he had and hooked on with a couple of independent league teams in 2003, the Selma Cloverleafs in Alabama (a team that had no home park and consequently played all its games on the road) and the Baton Rouge River Bats in Louisiana. Though no one felt a player just starting out at such an advanced age had much of a future, John-Henry hit .190 for the River Bats as a first baseman and DH. Wearing #30, the 6'5" 220-pound Williams's stats read:

AVG	G	AB	R	H	2B	3B	HR	RBI	BB	SO	SB	CS	SLG	OBP	E
2 Williams, John, DH .273	13	33	3	9	2	0	0	1	4	13	0	1	.333	.400	0
T Williams, John, 1B .153	26	72	3	11	3	0	0	2	9	33	0	2	.194	.274	4

The River Bats, interestingly, are owned by a retired United States Marine Corps colonel, Gilda Jackson, an African-American woman. The San Diego Padres invited three of the River Bats to the Arizona Fall League in 2003.

The River Bats won the 2003 South Eastern Professional Baseball League playoffs, but by the time they entered postseason competition, John-Henry was no longer with them. Something was wrong. He was becoming too fatigued. Come October, he was diagnosed with acute myelogenous leukemia, a particularly deadly form of the cancer. Less than six months after diagnosis, despite a bone marrow transplant from his sister Claudia, John-Henry Williams succumbed to cancer.

In 2014, Claudia wrote the book *Ted Williams, My Father*, which was in part a tribute to John-Henry and painted a far more sympathetic picture of her brother than had anyone else, even though she readily acknowledged that there was a dynamic between John-Henry and their father which excluded her. "I had a huge disadvantage," he wrote. "I was a girl."[240] Claudia's book offered a frank look at family life with Ted Williams – what it was like living with him, and learning to live without him, all of the time that Ted wasn't around.

Though John-Henry indeed did attract a great deal of negative ink and comment, many who knew Ted Williams saw how he could light up with pleasure seeing his son enter a room. A father may sometimes be blind to a son's faults, but there is little doubt that this father very much loved this son. It was not a relationship without difficult, but Ted really loved John-Henry. Ted hadn't made much time for John-Henry in the first couple of decades of his son's life, but he welcome John-Henry in his latter years. One of Ted's friends, Steve Brown, even found Ted counseling him on healing within his own family. "I got to witness John-Henry coming back in Ted's life. A lot of people don't realize that, but when John-Henry came back, Ted was the happiest man on the face of the earth. Even when John-Henry would disappoint him, it was a short-lived thing and Ted would be over it. A lot of people never got to see that side of him, but that was the parent John-Henry never had before."

Brown saw a parallel to Ted's relationship with his brother Danny. "Ted loved his brother despite what he did. He had the same kind of love for him he did John-Henry. He never saw the dark side. He knew it existed. He would even confront it as far as talking about it, but since he was not personally involved in their actions, he forgave them."

Ted even prompted a reconciliation within Brown's family. "Ted was responsible for myself and my son patching up our differences. He made me…Ted made me…he made me call my son. I was a hard-head like him, but he told me he was my son and I was my father. He had met my son Steve and he liked him, and so he physically called me on the carpet about it. He grilled me. Ted made me address [the problem between us] and get it out of the way. I thank him to this day because it was the best thing I could have done."[241]

Back to baseball.

Ted's uncles Saul, Paul and Bruno all played semipro baseball, as we have seen. Bruno's son Danny was on the championship Santa Barbara High School team and might have gone farther had he not had to take out a couple of years for the Korean War. The player in the next generation with the most talent, though, was Sal Herrera Jr.

Sal is Manuel Herrera's older brother, taken in by Rayo Hernandez after Sal Sr. had orphaned his children. Sal was scouted by a number of organizations and signed by the same scout who signed Eddie Mathews to the Braves. By all accounts, Sal had the tools. The problem was, he had a temper to match. Manuel explained, "Sal should have been a Hall of Famer – not because he was my brother, [but because] he had the tools. He had a temper and it caused him some big-time problems in baseball. You can not scream at the fans and run after them with a bat into the stands. He was built like Mickey Mantle but bigger and almost as fast as the Mick. He was so talented and strong, but he was tough as they come on others as well as himself. I got to see him play football in high school and no one on the opposing team could bring him down. He was a fullback and ran over people like an out-of-control freight train! I saw him drag three guys 15 yards before he was taken down – many times. I was only 11 years old, but how can a person forget his brother running over people as he did! The guy should have played pro football. He was offered a tryout with the Cleveland Browns, but was signed by Johnny Moore of the [Milwaukee] Braves shortly after the football offer." Sal bought a 1953 Mercury with the $1000.00 bonus money he got for signing with the Braves.[242]

Manuel explained more. "Sal came to live with us at about the eighth grade, the Venzor family and me and my twin sister Natalie. He was on his last leg before juvenile hall. He was in the 8th grade as I remember. Sal never spoke about the Rayo household or his school atmosphere. He was a great athlete, but his own worst enemy. Eddie Mathews and he played American Legion and High School ball together. Eddie said, he "wished he had Sal's power" – but that ol' attitude cut deep into his career. Sal played center field at Santa Barbara High School and was All-CIF first team. He came in second for player of the year which was won by Marty Keough, who was from the Claremont area and later played first base for the Cincinnati Reds. Sal was the MVP of the Pomona Tournament and the scouts pored over the house to sign him before he graduated from school." This was the same tournament that Ted Williams had starred in and Sal won the same honor Ted had: a CIF player of the year.

"'A waste of a complete baseball player' – those were the words of many a baseball player who played with or against Sal Herrera. I know because I asked about Sal's talent on the diamond. He was married at the age of 18 and left for baseball the day after. He was a scared kid when he left for baseball, but said, playing in the major leagues was so easy that he couldn't believe it! He beat out Hank Aaron and then beat himself out!"[243]

After baseball Sal got a job in the glass business where he graduated from an apprentice to journeyman and later served as a mechanic glazier. He was a supervisor for a large glass company and help build the MGM Grand Hotel, McCarran Airport, Brentwood Towers and many other high rises.

Gene Bowman confirms Manuel's story. Bowman was a pitcher, also signed by Johnny Moore. "Sal had all the talent in the world. Big, fast kid. Could run. Boy, he had the tools. I played with him in Boise. He was just always in trouble, though, fighting with the fans and everything else. He was a talent, but Johnny Moore finally just said he'd had enough. He was maybe four years or so younger than I was. One time he went down to Cabrillo Park in Santa Barbara and wanted Eddie [Mathews] to help him with his hitting. He was having trouble, so he got down there and Ed tried to help him but he turned to Eddie and said, 'Hey, I know more than that.' So Ed said, 'Well, so just tick with it.' He just wouldn't listen to anybody. Ed was nice to him. He said, 'OK, well, good luck to you.'"[244] Sal played some in Boise, some in Evansville, but never rose much higher than B ball.

Gabriel Arellanes signed with the Brooklyn Dodgers around the same time, and played for about five years in the Dodgers system – Texas League, California League, and the Midwest, Southern, and Eastern leagues. Arellanes was signed out of Santa Barbara High, too. He had tied Ted Williams' record in the Pomona tournament, hitting four home runs one year. He remembers Sal well: "Sal signed with the Braves a couple of years ahead of me. He got kicked out of the Braves chain - he punched the coach. Then the word was out, 'Hands off of Sal.' He had too much of a temper. He was a pretty tough hombre. We were all raised kind of tough. We all fought and boxed and everything else."[245]

Saul Venzor's grandson, Chaz's boy Greg, knew that he was related to Ted Williams. "We knew in elementary school," he told this author in February 2004. "We would tell our friends and they would just laugh at us." Who was going to believe that little Greg Venzor was related to the Hall of Fame baseball player? The family connection had never been publicized. Greg didn't even play baseball when he went through school, but for the last few years has served as head baseball coach for the junior varsity at Bishop Diego High School in Santa Barbara, and more recently at the city's Dos Pueblos High School. He's also assistant coach for the varsity baseball team.[246]

Greg himself has two sons Joshua and Jacob – Saul Venzor's great-grandsons – who both played middle infield and pitched a bit as well. Josh played at both schools, but did not play in college. Jacob currently plays at Dos Pueblos, and has some aspirations of trying to play college ball. Time will tell.

Ruth Gonzales, one of Ted's cousins, said, about Ted, "He didn't claim any relatives" (meaning that he kept his relatives at arm's length.) I asked about Ted's aunt Sarah Diaz, and she said that Sarah was the exception: "She was the only one that Ted wanted to see. Ted would tell Sarah, 'Don't tell anybody. If you do, I will never come and visit you again.' Some of her cousins, when May died, wanted to go, to see Ted Williams. He [arranged] a private funeral. They didn't say anything much about May; they just wanted to see Ted Williams."[247]

Ruth Gonzales's son David Gonzales played a little bit in high school, but David's son Davey Gonzalez actually starred when he was in high school.

Davey says he was about 12 or 13 when he first found that there was a family tie to Ted Williams. He wrote Ted in Islamorada and explained how he was related through his grandmother. He got back a nice note and a personalized photograph, which he has saved. Davey played third base for Downey High School and was team MVP in 1985, and a first-team C.I.F. All-Star selection – the same C.I.F. in which Ted had starred back in the mid-1930s. Davey played for the Norwalk Birds in 1986; the team entered and won the Connie Mack World Series in Farmington, New Mexico. At least one Williams relative was on a team what won a World Series! Davey went to USC and made the JV squad, but he gave priority to his studies and didn't keep at baseball.[248]

Ted's nephews Sam and Ted both played some Little League ball, but neither pursued the game. Ted's grand-nephew Noah Williams (11-year-old son of nephew Ted and Sue Stein) shows an interest in the game. Noah has played since T ball, really enjoys it, and loves playing first base. In 2002, he told this author that he wanted to be "the greatest hitter who ever lived." Must have heard that somewhere. Noah lives in Oakland, California and was fortunate to be drafted on the local Red Sox for the 2004 season, where he'll stay until he moves to the next level... but as his father says, "Ted Williams was a pretty special talent and it may not extend to the rest of us!"

ARELLANES, HERRERA GET TRYOUTS

Sal Herrera.

There's a Tom Venzor living in Schuyler, Nebraska. No known relation, but he's a Venzor, son of Armando Venzor, and in July 2003, he pitched the second game of a doubleheader between the towns of York and Schuyler. Unfortunately, he didn't win. We'll keep our ears peeled for more word of Tom Venzor.

Lastly, there is a Venzor long associated with baseball who lives in the Mexican state of Chihuahua, the state from which May Venzor's parents emigrated to the United States. Senor Jesus Manuel Ruiz Venzor is in his late 60s as of this writing, a baseball announcer very well known throughout Chihuahua. In 2002, the area's top amateur championship was named in his honor.

WAS TED WILLIAMS RELUCTANT TO TALK ABOUT HIS HISPANIC HERITAGE?

Was Ted Williams reluctant to talk about his Hispanic heritage? He didn't hesitate to touch on it in talking with John Underwood, but it only produced a line in passing. Nonetheless, Ted recognized that he "would have run into problems in those days" due to "the prejudices people had in Southern California." It may have been something he deliberately concealed during his playing days, and only felt comfortable acknowledging in later years.

It's a fair guess, of course, that his awareness of discrimination led to his welcoming of black players like Larry Doby, the first African-American in the American League, and to his ground-breaking induction speech at the Hall of Fame, calling for the inclusion of the great players from the Negro Leagues. On that occasion in 1966, Ted said, "Baseball gives every American boy a chance to excel. This is the nature of man and the name of the game. I hope that someday Satchel Paige and Josh Gibson will be voted into the Hall of Fame as symbols of the great Negro players who are not here only because they weren't given the chance."

Peter Gammons called it "the most important induction speech in history."[249]

Five years later, on accepting a Brotherhood Award at Howard University, Ted said, "As I look back on my career, I'm thankful that I was given the chance to play baseball; it's about the only thing I could do - and I've thought many a time, what would have happened to me if I hadn't had the chance. A chill goes up my back when I think I might have been denied this if I had been black."[250]

As a youth, Ted was clearly sensitive about his image. He was embarrassed by his mother being "out in the middle of the damn street all the time," about the fact that other kids had better clothing, about how skinny he was, about the house being "dirty all the time." When Eddie Collins came to visit, he was embarrassed that the family had to cover the hole in his chair "with a five-cent towel." Add the prejudice of others to the mix, and it wouldn't be surprising if Ted felt an inclination to distance himself from his mother's family's ethnicity. After Ted died, the executor of Ted Williams' estate said, "Ted didn't want anyone to know he was part Mexican. It concerned him. He was afraid they wouldn't let him play. He'd say, 'It was an entirely different time back then.'"[251]

Mary Herrera Redding knew the feeling: "At that time Spanish wasn't cool. Like the Indians here in Montana, they were punished for speaking their language and practicing their heritage."[252] As a youngster, Mary proactively tried to lighten her coloring so that she might be perceived a little more like the more favored Anglos around her. Raised by May's sister Jeanne, Mary was a sort of step-sister to Howard Winet. Dr. Winet remembered, "Mary might have had a little Aztec in her. She and Abby [Moreno] – this is something that used to fascinate me as a kid – they used to spend a lot of time peroxiding their arms. This is something that was done by a lot of Latinos, because they wanted to look like gringos. The dark hair would give them away. They thought it was heavy dark hair on their arms – I didn't think it was heavy, but they did – and they were busy at least once a week peroxiding their arms. I was fascinated by it.[253]

Connie Matthews, reflected, "Ted...it seems to me now Ted did not like to associate with part of the family, the Hernandez family. He didn't want to be associated with the dark part of the family, which was part of the Hernandezes, Manuel especially. I think he married a very dark woman and most of the kids are dark. Right away you know that they are part Indian or whatever. They're dark. And I know that Ted always....'Don't bring any [of them around.]'"[254] Skin color was, rather typically for the era, a topic of some conversation. Connie remembers Sarah Diaz being "kind of catty" about one of the Venzors, asking, "How come this Venzor, he was so dark?" Connie's sister Ruth agrees: "He didn't want to associate with his relatives, and I don't blame him. He didn't like any of us relatives. Partly, he didn't want anyone to know that he was of Mexican descent."[255]

Ted was angry about one thing that happened when he was waiting for an offer from one of the teams who had scouted him. Ted's cousin Madeline Cordero and his Aunt Sarah Diaz were both staying at the Utah Street house, and they knew that May didn't want Ted to get signed. He was too young, she felt, and she didn't want him to be heading East to play baseball, so she asked them to hide the mail. "Ted's waiting for that letter. A few days go by, a week goes by. Ted's getting impatient. Asks the mailman. Turns out Madeline hid the letter because May didn't want Ted to go. When Ted found out, he shouted, 'You damn Indian, go back to the reservation!'"[256]

Maybe there were good days and there were bad days. Matters of race and ethnicity have always been charged. David Ronquillo recounts a story told him recently by Priscilla Wade, another relative. "Priscilla describes this large group of family that goes to meet him at the train station. Here's this unsuspecting 19-year-old kid – maybe 20 – he's been told by the Red Sox, don't let anyone know you're Hispanic. Time and place. Being Hispanic at that time was not something that you want to embrace. There was a lot of discrimination. He doesn't look Hispanic. He's got the last name Williams. Who's going to know he's Hispanic?

"So he sees this whole family coming toward him. He doesn't know what to do. He panics and does a U-turn! Does a 180. Walks away from them. It was as though it happened yesterday. Priscilla was telling us about it and she's saying, "I am STILL mad at him for doing that!"

"The guy didn't know what to do. He was panic-stricken."[257]

He was aware that if he'd been seen as Hispanic, it could have caused difficulties for him? "There's no question about it. That's what I think. That was a very significant crossroads in his life.

"This is speculative on my part but I think it's pretty reasonable speculation. Ted was, I think, embarrassed about his mom's connection with the Salvation

Army. But I think he was also somewhat embarrassed by his Hispanic roots. Here you have this guy who's 6'4". He doesn't look in the least bit Hispanic. He has the name Williams so no one's ever going to suspect that he's Hispanic. May was

Noah Williams, son of nephew Ted, plays first base in the North Oakland/South Oakland Little League. Coincidentally, he was drafted onto the Red Sox, 2004, where he'll play until he moves to the next level.

a very attractive woman. I don't know how Hispanic she looked. I've seen many, many photographs, and I saw her, but I don't have a recollection of her looking Hispanic."[258]

"If it's not popular to be Hispanic today, my goodness, at that time it was a death knell."[259]

Throughout the extended family, English was the language of those of both May's and Ted's generations. In El Paso, Ruth Gonzales and her family spoke both languages in the home, "but mostly English. Micaela [May Williams], the same. She would speak Spanish to her mother and my mother, but to her kids and sisters and her brothers, she would speak English."[260] There may simply not have been as much self-awareness or self-consciousness about ethnicity in those days. Ruth's niece – Ernest Ponce's daughter -- Maureen Surratt comments, "There were no hyphenating Americans when I grew up."[261]

Danny told his sons that Ted called the Santa Barbara family, "the Mexicans." Danny wasn't raised Hispanic, either. "My father never took on the Hispanic lifestyle, never made mention of it. I think he was happy to have come from an English father. I realize in retrospect he totally looks Mexican. I'm sure for Ted it was a bit of an embarrassment. It was maybe considered lower class, or working class, or peasant. Certainly they were peasant-type people. Not that there's anything negative in that; it was just their life. They were pretty much immigrants. I think that's the exciting part of the story."[262] May, though, was probably not herself viewed as Hispanic. "When I lived with May, you never got the sense that they were Hispanic, or that there were any of those influ-ences. It just seemed pretty everyday and normal. In Santa Barbara, though, they are tortillas and beans, and cooked food like that. I think May maybe moved more out of it than the others did, maybe because she didn't stay with them.'"[263]

In Santa Barbara, of course, there was a lot of Spanish spoken. Teresa Cor-dero Contreras talks about her grandmother Natalia Venzor. "She spoke a little bit of English. She'd answer the phone, "Jeannie no here" or "Sarah no here." She understood. I didn't speak any Spanish and when I went over to Grandma's, I'd just say, "Hi Grandma" and give her a great old big hug and a kiss, and outside I went. My dad spoke a lot of English, and my mom, too. The only time I ever heard them speak Spanish is when they didn't want us to know. Then you try to learn but it's hard."[264]

Ted probably heard a lot of Spanish around him, but being a young boy, sim-ply tuned out. And May's ministry was in the Salvation Army in San Diego, and it was not an Hispanic ministry. The Salvation Army photographs we see of her often show her posed with figures of the Anglo establishment. As we have noted as well, Sarah Diaz and other family members emphasized that the family roots were European, not Mexican.

"Mexicans can truly be more discriminatory toward darker-skinned people than we are in this country toward black people," David Ronquillo interject-ed. "It's not even close. It's incredible. In Mexico, one of the reasons that men began wearing mustaches is to distinguish themselves as not being of Indian blood. People in Mexico who had Spanish heritage, as do I from my father's side, it was like a real premium to have, for example, light-colored eyes, or light-colored hair and particularly light-colored skin."

David illustrates with a modest personal experience from the time he spent living as a student in Mexico. "One day we're out...this is mid-Sixties in Mexico. We go out and buy these sandals from a vendor on the street, the kind with tire treads. There were three of us students who lived with a family, and the woman was highly offended that we bought them because it reflected something that the Indians wore. Sarah would have said this, because my grandmother – who was May and Sarah's aunt – used to wear dark dresses with a white blouse. The Basque look. My grandmother was very light-complected, as was my mother. A lot of Mexican people say, 'I'm from Spain' because they want to distance themselves from the Indian part of the Mexican culture as much as they can."[265]

As it happens the family ethnicity was quite mixed. There were *indios* in the family, and most of the family understood the primary roots to be Basque, but more than one relative spoke of Russian background. Esther Slagle talked of it (see above, in a footnote) and so did Ruth Ponce Gonzales: "My sister tells me that they had Russian blood in there somewhere. Santiago and Eduviges were blond and blue-eyed. They looked Russian. [Natalia Venzor] had golden honey brown hair. My dad's ancestors were probably from France. It was all a mixture. On my mother's side, they had some Russian ancestors. My mother was very white but she had brown hair and brown eyes. All the others were blond *gueros*. My sister was a blonde. I was a brunette.'"[266]

Did Ted Williams truly turn his back on his Hispanic heritage, or was it mostly irrelevant to him? Is it something we focus on more today than people would have in his years of growing up? Probably some of each. Joe Villarino, Ted's schoolboy friend and Hoover High teammate, had a Mexican father and a Spanish mother, and he knew Ted from third grade on. This is how Joe put it: it was "not that he didn't want to be known as a Mexican, but it just wasn't part of his life."[267] Leigh Montville, researching Ted's life for his biography Ted Williams, spoke with Ted's second wife, Lee Howard, at some length. She said "he never ever talked about it when they were married."[268] He truly may not have seen it that important a part of his life. As Ted recognized, having the last name Williams and being raised largely in an Anglo environment no doubt facilitated his acceptance in organized baseball in the 1930s. This lack of focus on his Hispanic heritage may have been convenient, but it may not have been so calculated.

Joe Villarino's perception may have hit the nail on the head – Ted was raised an Anglo and grew up almost entirely in Anglo environments. There are very few seemingly Latino surnames in his high school yearbook. Frank Cushing, who used to shag balls at Hoover, came to know Ted later in life as a fellow Marine. Of Ted's mother, he said, "You would have never known May had any Mexican [blood.] I didn't know it until years later. [Ted] didn't talk about it very much, but he wasn't ashamed of it. He would remark a little about it – why he liked guacamole or so forth. "I guess it's the Mexican in me," or some remark like that. He didn't try to hide it."[269] It is undeniable, though, that he quietly welcomed Larry Doby with dignity; Doby was the first African-American in the American League.

Doby said, "When I first got in the League in '47, he was one of the few people who said 'hello' and said 'good luck.' Him and Dom DiMaggio and a fellow named Rudy York. The thing that impressed me about Ted is that… with some people you can feel sincerity. With other people, you can feel it was politics, or something.

"During that time you left your glove on the field, and you'd pass the out-fielders on the way on & off the field. He'd just say, 'Congratulations, good luck.' [He just gave me a feeling of being welcome, which was important to me] especially when you had a lot of other people not saying anything. It was not a 'welcome' thing. I don't think he was that sort of person [to make a spectacle of it], just a quiet kind of person, going about his business. Didn't have to make any big deal out of it. That's why I feel it was from the heart."[270]

Ted also went out of his way to welcome Pumpsie Green, the first Red Sox African-American, choosing him as his partner for tossing the ball on the side while warming up before the game. He made no pronouncement on the subject. Again, he made his point with quiet, even elegant, dignity. Ted did have a feeling for those at a disadvantage – be they kids who got cancer or those who suffered discrimination.

Ted not only crusaded for Negro League players to be brought into the Hall of Fame. He also spoke up for Native Americans, a few years earlier, in December 1962. Reacting to a *New York Times* editorial, Williams angrily wrote in his syndicated weekly column, "The Indians in this country, as usual, are getting the shaft...They're still treated here as the scum of the earth as if they're being punished for being here when all of us first came over. I would think that after all these years, with all the assimilation that has taken place between all our people, that the Indians certainly should have their place in society. But we look the other way. The only good Indian is a dead Indian, still seems to be the motto." He went on to argue that we're spending millions in foreign aid, and CARE sends packages to other lands, but maybe it was time that the Peace Corps did something for American Indians who "can't even belong to a country which they once owned."[271]

Ted returned to the theme in February 1964 with a column headlined "Lo, the Poor Indian Off the Diamond" in the February 16, 1964 *Houston Post*. Both columns complained that only the Cleveland Indians, Milwaukee Braves, and Washington Redskins were treated as first-class citizens, but not the American Indian. "I know that there are many people who feel as keenly as I do about the terrible treatment of our people and the word 'our' should be underlined...And it's about time we start making amends to our own people." Ted noted that the average American Indian life span was 42 years, not the 62 years of other Americans, and that the average education was only through eighth grade. "If you're a real American, you should be angry, insulted that this kind of treatment has been allowed for so many years.... Why don't we all really begin acting like sports and start off by giving back to the American Indian their dignity and place in the human race? It belongs to them the same way it belongs to us. It's our shame when it should be our glory."

These two columns, which appeared nationally years before his famous Hall of Fame speech, have never attracted attention but, in retrospect, foreshadow Ted Williams' willingness to speak out on the issue of prejudice and fair treatment. Knowing a favored uncle who was directly descended from the

Chumash Indians may have infused his words with additional passion. And growing up in a family of diverse backgrounds may have sensitized Ted to the issue in general.

A TRULY AMERICAN FAMILY

Although his family roots are many and diverse, Ted Williams' family was truly an American family. Almost all of us are of immigrant background. Many of us are of mixed roots and many of us truly do not know the full story of our own heritage, even going back just three or four generations. Ted Williams was born and raised in a fascinating, lively, vital family with no shortage of personalities. With family roots in Wales and England, and in Mexico and the Basque country, Ted came from a truly American family which covered the gamut, as we noted at the start: cavalrymen and cowboys, longshoremen and photographers, evangelists and more. And from this context was produced a man the likes of whom we may never see again - a crusader against cancer in children, a world-class fisherman, a United States Marines jet pilot, and the man who many feel was the greatest hitter who ever lived.

RECOGNITION OF TED WILLIAMS, LATINO

As noted above, it was Manuel Herrera reaching out to Jim Prime after publication of the book *Ted Williams: A Tribute*, and the lengthy interviews I conducted with him and Ted's aunt Sarah Diaz in 1999, which eventually led to "El Splinter Esplendido, Ted Williams's Latino Heritage," the column I wrote for the *Boston Globe Magazine*, which was publishing on June 2, 2002, just about a month before Ted Williams' death. ("La Astilla Esplendida" wouldn't have translated as well to a New England readership.) I had fortunately had the opportunity to speak with Ted himself and have him confirm some of this first-hand, including his memory of Saul Venzor.

In researching the family history, I had been in touch with a number of people over the years from 1999 to 2002, visiting Ernesto Ponce and Kathleen Osowski in El Paso and so forth. One of the people with whom I was in touch was Gabriel "Tito" Avila, Jr. He founded the Hispanic Heritage Baseball Museum and Hall of Fame in San Francisco in 1999, and the Museum inducted its inaugural class at a banquet/dance at the Grand Hyatt Hotel in San Francisco on February 23, 2002. The honorees were Orlando Cepeda, Tito Fuentes, Minnie Miñoso, and Ted Williams. Ted himself was in the hospital in Florida and, naturally, unable to attend. I had the true honor of accepting on behalf of Ted Williams. I was presented with a "number 9" jersey with "Hispanic Heritage Baseball Museum" on the front and "Williams 9" on the back. I sent the jersey to the Ted Williams Museum, located now in Tropicana Field but at the time in Hernando, Florida, just blocks from Ted's home. I found myself dancing next to Orlando Cepeda, an experience that was – in its own way – something like my dancing next to Mick Jagger in Rotterdam in 1982.

Tito Avila, noting the forthcoming 20th anniversary of the Hispanic Heritage Baseball Museum Hall of Fame, said in January 2018 that to date the Museum Hall of Fame has inducted 67 inductees and 16 pioneers. "The Museum Hall of Fame is very proud to have inducted Ted Williams as its first inductee. Ted Williams was an American Hero who served our country twice and made us proud on and off the field. The Hispanic Heritage Baseball Museum Hall of Fame Board of Directors felt that Ted Williams was not only a hero but a symbol of a true American patriot not only playing the field but giving back to the community."[272]

Over the next couple of years, I helped organize a few events to honor Ted Williams – in Boston (at the Boston Public Library), in Cooperstown (at the National Baseball Hall of Fame), and in San Diego. The event in San Diego was held at the Hall of Champions, the Balboa Park facility started by Ted's high school and lifelong friend, Bob Breitbard. On March 29, 2003, a couple of hundred people gathered for a day of papers and reminiscences, the event titled "The Kid from San Diego - A Celebration of Ted Williams."

We were fortunate to be joined by major-league ballplayers Ray Boone, Jerry Coleman, Jack Harshman, and Max West.

PAPERS WERE PRESENTED OR APPRECIATIONS OF TED WERE RENDERED BY THE FOLLOWING:

Tom Larwin, San Diego SABR, offered welcoming remarks and some thoughts on Ted Williams.

Bob Breitbard (president of Ted's graduating class at Hoover High School, San Diego, and currently founder and President Emeritus of the San Diego Hall of Champions, which hosted the event) offered some memories of Ted.

Bob Boynton, "57 Years Separated My Two Meetings with Ted Williams."

I chaired a panel on Ted's childhood friends and his neighborhood; this panel embraced the next three presentations.

Les Cassie Jr., Joe Villarino, and Bob Breitbard took part in a panel of Ted's boyhood friends and high school teammates. Joe Villarino, age 84, had just played softball the day before, and got a single! Baseball is in the blood.

G. Jay Walker presented images and discussion on "Early Years in North Park."

Dennis Donley, librarian at Hoover High School, discussed their collection and the researchers who have visited Hoover over the years. Dennis also talked a bit about how Ted is sometimes invoked by current coaches at Hoover.

I presented some research information both on Ted's play while at Hoover, and then chaired a panel on Ted's relatives, with emphasis on his Hispanic heritage.

A very remarkable part of the conference was that I was able to convene thirty-three (yes, 33) relatives of Ted Williams attended, who came to the event from various parts of the State of California. Nephews and cousins and the like. Three relatives - Frank Venzor, Dee Venzor Allen, and Ted Williams (a nephew of Ted, his brother Danny's son) were on a panel discussing Ted and his family.

John Holway presented some thoughts on "The Unknown Ted" - a variety of facts he uncovered over the years, including Ted's horoscope from the time of his birth.

Fred O. Rodgers presented "Ted's 1941 Season as Captured by *The Sporting News*" - with illustrative clips from the pages of *TSN*.

Todd W. Anton presented "For Love of Country: Duty, Honor, Baseball" - a discussion of Ted's military history.

John Bolthouse, archivist for the San Diego Aerospace Museum, discussed "Ted's Aircraft and Equipment."

Andy Strasberg and Roger Engle discussed "Ted's Baseball Camp." Andy showed a number of photographs from his year at the camp and evoked envy in almost all of us, and Roger showed home movies of the camp which his parents Ann & Roy Engle had taken. Roger's brother Dave Engle became

Venzor and Hernandez family gathering, August, 1928.

a major-league ballplayer. Having been a front office man for the Padres, Andy,

too, made it from the Ted Williams Camp to major-league baseball.

Carlos Bauer presented the speculative "What If Ted Had Stayed Home?" (and played for the PCL Padres.)

Frank Myers offered "How Ted Williams Became A Padre" offering fact and hypotheses regarding Ted's signing with the home town team.

Dan Boyle detailed "1936: Ted Williams' Professional Debut" - a focus on Ted's first year with the San Diego Padres

Bill Swank followed with "Ted Williams, Earl Keller, and the 1937 San Diego Padres"

James D. Smith III offered "'The Kid' Leaves Home: Ted Williams and the 1938 Minneapolis Millers"

The highlight, in a certain way, was the assembling of the 33 relatives of Ted Williams, all from the Latino side of the family (see the photograph elsewhere in this book): Peggy Amidon, Judi (Amidon) Vista, Linda Amidon, Louie Mata, Louie Mata III, Mari Mata, Mitchell Amidon, Virginia Amidon, Jackie Mata, Bill Amidon, Suzy Amidon, James Amidon, Ron Amidon, Nicholas Atondo, David C. Allen, Frank Venzor, Alyse Amidon, Dee (Venzor) Allen, Geno Lucero, Erich Venzor, Hugo Nathan Gaytan, Gudrun Venzor, David Ronquillo, Chaz Venzor, Ted Williams, Rose (Venzor) Larson, Karma Barber, Bob Larson, Teresa (Cordero) Contreras, Dan Williams Jr., Carrie (Venzor) Ortiz, Fred S. Contreras, and Carl Jean Contreras.

Todd Anton and I later collaborated on a couple of books – *When Baseball Went to War* and *When Football Went to War.*

Several of the participants, and others, contributed to the book *The Kid: Ted Williams in San Diego* (published by Rounder Books in 2005), which contained an earlier version of this text.

Awareness that Ted Williams had been Latino began to spread. The National Baseball Hall of Fame offered a tee-shirt for a while that listed Latino Hall of Famers, with Ted Williams top of the list. But then a minor controversy arose in August 2005, wherein Major League Baseball didn't seem to have gotten the message. Richard Sandomir led a story in the *New York Times* writing, "When Major League Baseball unveiled its ballot for the Latino Legends team Tuesday, the 60 nominees excluded two of the greatest Hispanic players ever: Ted Williams and Reggie Jackson." [273] MLB argued that neither were publicly linked to their Latino heritage, that they didn't "represent the Latin community." Sandomir wrapped up his article: "Jackson, whose grandmother was Puerto Rican, said he is 'proud of my Latin blood,' but not upset at being left off the ballot. But he is offended by any suggestion by baseball about his connection to those roots. 'They have no right to pass judgment on what I claim about my Latin heritage,' said Jackson, whose middle name is Martinez. 'I just don't run my mouth off about it.'"

What was MLB's rationale? J.A. Marzán explained: "Sandomir cited Carmine Tiso, a baseball 'spokesperson,' who explained that lineage is not baseball's standard for identifying a player as Hispanic: '[Baseball]... applied a litmus test that went beyond statistics: the nominees had to have a direct connection to their Latino heritage.' A second cited spokesman, Richard Levin, said the players should 'represent the Latin community.' Tiso added a defense of Williams: 'It's not that he was ashamed of his heritage, but we felt that we didn't find enough connection from Ted to that Latino heritage.' Levin appended an additional consideration: that Williams's name 'would distort the ballot' and 'cause havoc' because his ethnicity is not widely known."[274]

One could mock the notion of resultant "havoc," but the explanation offered by the Major League Baseball spokesmen shares similarity to that later argued by scholar Adrian Burgos Jr. that Ted Williams should not be considered as Latino because he "did not identify as Latino nor was he racialized as such during his legendary career."[275] Ted hadn't had to Anglicize his surname, suffer ridicule for his accent, or bear discrimination at contract time.

Ted Williams was able to live as Anglo – fairly easily, since he'd been largely raised as such. If he didn't publicly identify as Latino, does that disqualify him from being considered Latino? We have the evidence that Ted knew he could have been considered Latino ("If I had had my mother's name, there is no doubt I would have run into problems in those days, the prejudices people had in Southern California.") As we have seen throughout this book, it is clear he was well aware of "the Mexicans" in his family. It's reasonable to conclude that he *did* identify as partially Latino – but, for a cluster of reasons, informed by time and place, wanted to avoid that perception.

Burgos further argues that "it is also important that we do not rewrite the history of Latinos and baseball by retroactively inserting Williams because he chose not to do so on the grandest platform he was provided." That platform was the occasion of his 1966 induction into the National Baseball Hall of Fame. Ted talked about the playground director who'd worked with him as a kid, his coach in high school, and other influences. He could have made something of his Latino heritage, but he did not. The absence of this ac-knowledgement could be considered underscored by his use of the bully pul-pit to call for the recognition of Satchel Paige and Josh Gibson as "symbols of the great Negro players who are not here only because they weren't given the chance." Here was an opportunity for Williams to state what he, three years later, expressed in *My Turn At Bat*, that he himself *could have* suffered from prejudice. One could perhaps understand that he wasn't ready to throw open windows in public that he had long been accustomed to keeping closed. One could even argue that – had he been tempted – he might have preferred not to muddy the waters, the better to keep the focus on his point about the Negro Leaguers. They *had* suffered discrimination; he had not had to.

Needless to say, it's a complex question. There is identity, and there is public acknowledgment of identity. If one wants to avoid being "branded" as of such-and-such a heritage, the human psyche is such that one can even deny something to the point where one's own consciousness is deceived by the masking and denial. Williams never denied he was Latino; he just didn't want to go there. Had he been born a couple of decades later, or lived a decade or two longer, this might have been otherwise.

MLB itself had perhaps changed its tune by 2012. On September 25, 2012 during Hispanic Heritage Month, Jesse Sanchez, a writer for MLB.com, released his "All-Time Latino Team."[276]

Full-length biographies by Leigh Montville (in 2004) and Ben Bradlee, Jr. (in 2013) helped better establish the popular awareness of this side of Ted Williams' ancestry.

A TRIP TO MEXICO

In 2010, an opportunity to visit the area where Ted's maternal grandparents were born and raised was presented to when Ricardo Urquidi Espinoza of Hidalgo del Parral, Chihuahua, invited me to come to Chihuahua to speak at two different events – an evening gathering of sportswriters in the city of Chihuahua itself and then a "Conferencia Historica" on the Patio Central de la Presidencia Municipal on July 10, 2010 in the city of Hidalgo del Parral. Ricardo is a sportswriter himself, and we had corresponded by email on the subject. I'd sent him a complimentary copy of *The Kid: Ted Williams in San Diego*. When the invitation was formalized, I asked Ted's nephew Ted to see if he wanted to come. He did, and he was welcomed by Ricardo, and added to both programs.

As a bonus, Ricardo took us to see a Mexican League baseball team. The Parral team has been a perennial championship team and won again that night.

We took a sidetrip to the village of Valle de Allende, from whence Federico Ponce came, the village where May Williams' uncle had been administrator. As best we can pin down, this was the home of the Venzor and Ponce families. We met with local genealogists and historians there, and a couple of Venzors, too!

We had a wonderful few days, visiting Ricardo's family at home, and meeting any number of people interested in the story. Ted returned home to Oakland, to his wife Sue Stein and son Noah. I took advantage of being in Chihuahua to fulfill a longtime dream and booked a ride on "El Chepe" – the Copper Canyon train, the Chihuahua al Pacifico Railway. I didn't go all the way to Los Mochis, but decided instead to just go as far as El Fuerte, Sinaloa and then return, spending a night at Divisadero in a wonderful hotel with a balcony that looked into the Copper Canyon. In El Fuerte, I stayed at Hotel Posada del Hidalgo, a hotel which had been built from the former home of Zorro – and I actually met "Zorro" himself (in this case, the lead singer of a very good *conjunto* who dressed in full Zorro costume for his performance.)

So it was Ted Williams to Zorro, quite an adventure.

As it happens, I also wrote Ted Williams' last words.

For several years, I edited Ted Williams Magazine for the Ted Williams Museum, and each year there was a message from Ted himself welcoming attendees to the annual event, which had come to embrace the induction of honorees into the Hitters Hall of Fame. Basically, I was Ted's ghostwriter for the last two or three years of the publication. I would write something and then send it for approval. Never was a word changed. Now that I look back on it, I should have had a little fun with it and added a phrase in Spanish.

Here was the final welcome:

INDUCTION 2002 –
A PERSONAL WELCOME FROM TED WILLIAMS

Looking back on 2001, I want to say that we have an awful lot to be thankful for.

I say that, though this has been a very difficult year for me. One word sums up a lot of my feelings about the last year: perseverance. I needed it as a ballplayer and I sure had to call on it during these last twelve months.

It's been a long year and a trying year and certainly the longest slump that Teddy Ballgame has ever been in! I had to persevere all year long and it's been a battle at times. Most of all, though, I am grateful - really and deeply grateful - to everybody who persevered with me through this time.

It has been a difficult year for the American people as well and for our many friends in other lands. My cap is off to the brave rescue personnel in New York, Washington, and Pennsylvania, to the passengers who fought back on that United Airlines flight and to our leaders and military who have responded appropriately and with determination.

Family means a lot in times like these. My family has been with me throughout. John-Henry has been by my side all year long and you couldn't ask for a more supportive son. Claudia pinch-hit for me at the 2001 induction and hit a grand slam. She's been terrific all year.

And my friends. Boy, the thing I missed most were my friends. I know so many of you have called. I've been glad to have the chance to talk with some of you, but I wish I could have spoken with all of you. Your love and support means so much to me.

I've had a few people come visit, too. Happy doesn't describe how I felt seeing my old friends Dominic DiMaggio and Johnny Pesky show up on my doorstep. They both drove all the way down from Boston to see me. After having me drive them in all these years, it was nice to have them return the favor. Those were a couple of wonderful days.

One of the bright spots in this otherwise difficult time was my induction into the Atlantic Salmon Hall of Fame. Some of my happiest memories were of fishing that river with my great friend Roy Curtis and now we are reunited in that great hall of fame.

I've been looking forward to the 2002 induction ceremonies. I worked on the selection of the hitters and the other award winners and I am so pleased to be able to honor some of the players I admired. Roger Maris - what a power hitter! And Don Mattingly - "Donnie Ballgame" - wow! Of course, my old friend Enos Slaughter from my days as a player - this guy could hit AND run! And Dwight Evans of the Red Sox - what a great player he was!

Barry Bonds and Jason Giambi both won the award they named after me for the second year in a row. I like that. Consistency. That's a big word for me, too.

Al Kaline. He says I helped him out with a couple of pointers. That kid didn't need any help from me. What talent he had as a hitter!

Now let me tell you about Gaylord Perry. I'm sure glad I never had to try to get a hit off him! Virgil Trucks, now I did hit a few off him. But I'll tell you, Trucks and Feller were the fastest two pitchers I ever faced.

I'm looking forward to seeing my good friend Tommy Lasorda again. I've missed him.

I hope you all enjoy yourselves this year and I just want to close by repeating one thing I left you with last year: I really do know how lucky I've been in my life. Get a good pitch to hit!

Natalia with Santiago and Rayo

PHOTO CREDITS

Dee V. Allen: 70, 116, 119, 143, 189

Ron Amidon: 36, 62, 64, 73, 90, 98, 100, 197

Alice Cooper: 63

Ruth Gonzales: 69

Manuel Herrera: 10, 11 (top), 101, 157

Rosalie Larson: 134

Tom Larwin: 156

Bill Nowlin: 41, back cover

San Diego Historical Society: 46

Maureen Surratt: 11 (bottom), 12, 18

Daniel Venzor: 136, 137, 139

Claudia Williams: 90

Daniel A. Williams, Jr. and Jan Williams: 162

May Williams Collection: front cover, 6, 15, 18, 21, 26, 28, 35, 38, 42, 43, 50, 52, 60, 76, 80, 82, 83, 85, 86, 94, 111, 113, 124, 129, 130, 153, 160, 165, 166, 168

Ted Williams (nephew): 29, 34, 39, 163, 181, 190

END NOTES

1   Author interview with Ernest "Joe" Villarino, May 9, 1997.

2   Communication from John Underwood, December 12, 2002.

3   Ed Linn, *Hitter*, 74.

4   Ernest Ponce obituary, El Paso Times, March 17, 2002.

5   Bill Nowlin, "Ted and Cuba," Ted Williams Magazine, February 2004. A slightly adapted version of the story was reprinted in Cuba in 2014 in Universo Beisbol (Ano 5, Numero 55, October 2014), 42-43.

6   Jim Prime & Bill Nowlin, Ted Williams: The Pursuit of Perfection, 57.

7   Linn, 121.

8   *My Turn At Bat*, 30.

9   Leigh Montville, *Ted Williams*, 19.

10   Michael Seidel, Ted Williams: A Baseball Life, 63.

11   Boston Globe, April 7, 1954.

12   My Turn At Bat, 30.

13   Ibid.

14   Communication from Peter Morris, April 9, 2004.

15   Boston Transcript, April 12, 1939. Presumably, Sam Williams' friend was named Ted.

16   My Turn At Bat, 31.

17   Ibid.

18   Thanks to Emil Rohracker of the 14th Cavalry Association for this information.

19   K. Bruce Galloway, *West Point: America's Power Fraternity* (New York: Simon & Schuster, 1973).

20   *My Turn At Bat*, 30.

21   Communication from Kimberly Mack, Salvation Army Museum of the West, December 3, 2002. How did May end up so far north, in Petaluma?

22   Author interview with Manuel Herrera, May 29, 1999. Manuel himself was raised as a Salvationist and remains deeply impressed to this day with May's commitment to the cause.

23   *Boston Globe*, August 29, 1961.

24   Communication from Kimberly Mack, December 3, 2002.

25   Author interview with Sarah Diaz, op. cit.

26   Linn, Hitter, op. cit, 30; My Turn At Bat, op. cit., 19.

27   Communication from Manuel Herrera, July 19, 2004.

28   Author interview with Edward Donovan, April 7, 2001.

29   Author interview with Ted Williams, April 28, 2000.

30   Ben Bradlee, Jr., The Kid: The Immortal Life of Ted Williams (New York: Little, Brown and Company, 2013), 33-35.

31   Linn, Hitter, op. cit., 34.

32   Williams' position was confirmed by a librarian in the California State Library's Government Publications Section who checked the State telephone directories for 1937 and 1939 and found him listed as jail inspector in the Department of Social Welfare. Communication from Catherine Hanson-Tracy, California State Library, December 23, 2003.

33   Interview with Teresa Cordero Contreras, May 28, 2000. Manuel Herrera recalled Samuel driving an old Essex. After the divorce, May would come to Santa Barbara on the Southern Pacific.

34   Author interview with Sarah V. Diaz, May 1999.

35   Linn, Hitter, op. cit., 34.

36   Ibid., 72. Mickie Frank, a member of Minnie's church recalls the house as "real sweet, very tiny. I would say modest." Author interview with Mickie Frank, January 5, 2003.

37   My Turn At Bat, op. cit., 29.

38   "Solon Economy Puts State Jail Inspector Out of Job," press clipping bureau excerpt from the Fresno Bee & Republican, July 12, 1939.

39   Samuel S. Williams, "Report on Proceedings, Sixty-Eighth Annual Congress of the American Prison Association," October 14, 1938.

40   Author interview with Alice Psaute, February 2003.

41   *My Turn At Bat*, 29.

42   Author interview with Manuel Herrera, May 1999.

43   Ibid.

44   Author interview with Alice Psaute, op. cit.

45   My Turn At Bat, 28.

46   Ibid., 29, 33.

47   Linn, *Hitter*, 73. In My Turn at Bat, Ted wrote, "I never wore a uniform or anything, but I was right at that age when a kid starts worrying about what other kids might think, especaially a gawky introverted kid like me, and I was just so ashamed." See page 28.

48   Author interview with Alice Psaute, op. cit.

49   Williams, My Turn At Bat, 28.

50   Linn, 29.

51   *My Turn At Bat*, 32.

52   "'Army' Recruiting Station? Perhaps -- To Assist Police," San Diego Sun, February 3, 1936.

53   San Diego Union, February 2, 1936.

54   "Handling Transients," editorial, San Diego Sun, February 1936.

55   Communication from Ted Williams, October 25, 2002.

56   *San Diego Union*, July 7, 1980.

57   Author interview with Alice Psaute, February 2003.

58   Clippings placed in scrapbook maintained by Alice Fries King.

59   Author interviews with Mickie Frank and Larry Frank, January 2003.

60   Communication from Manuel Herrera, June 16, 2002.

61   Author interview with Sarah Diaz, May 1999.

62   Communication from Manuel Herrera, May 1, 2000.

63   Interview with Mary Ponce, April 26, 2000. Eulalia Ponce, born in Mexico, lived in downtown Los Angeles near USC on Santa Barbara Street. Manuel Herrera knew her, and tells of her sad end, mugged going to the bank. "She was attacked while near a bus stop and was in a coma for several days then passed away. The thief took only $5 and also took her life." She died of a blood clot on January 3, 1971 at age 91. Her husband Federico had died of a heart attack at 78. Communication from Manuel Herrera, May 2, 2000, and interview with Ruth Gonzales, February 28, 2003.

64   Author interview with Ernesto Ponce, November 8, 2000.

65   Author interview with Sarah Diaz, May 1999.

66   Author interviews with Connie Matthews, November 26 and December 10, 2002.

67   Author interview with Connie Matthews, December 10, 2002.

68   Author interview with Ernest & Mary Ponce, November 8, 2000. Mary was clear – they never really saw May.

69   Author interview with Sarah Diaz, May 1999.

70   Author interview with Mary Ponce, April 26, 2000.

71   Author interview with Sarah Diaz, May 1999.

72   Author interview with David Ronquillo, October 23 & November 24, 2003.

73   Communication from Manuel Herrrera, May 31, 1999.

74   Author interview with Geno Lucero, September 2003.

75   Author interview with Esther Slagle, October 21, 2003.

76   Author interview with Connie Matthews, December 10, 2002.

77   Communication from Manuel Herrera, May 20, 2000.

78   Author interview with Ruth Gonzales, February 28, 2003.

79   Communication from Manuel Herrera, May 16, 2000.

80   Author interview with Sarah Diaz, May 1999.

81   Stephen Lawton, *Santa Barbara's Flying A Studio* (Santa Barbara: Fithian Press, 1997), 45.

82   Author interview with Sarah Diaz, May 1999.

83   Communication from Manuel Herrera, May 16, 2000.

84   Communication from Manuel Herrera, January 23, 2002.

85   Communication from Manuel Herrera, September 3, 2001.

86   Communication from Manuel Herrera, December 27, 2000.

87   Author interview with Manuel Herrera, May 29, 1999.

88   Communication from Manuel Herrera, May 20, 2000. Danny Venzor confirms the story. Similarly named for their Uncle Daniel, Bruno's son Danny remembers that Danny Williams and the "young gal" actually stayed on the living room couch at his house, 1006 Chino -- a house Danny still owns today as a rental. "Come to find out that she was underage. He picked her up someplace down south, and they were going to charge him with statutory rape." Author interview with Danny Venzor, December 28, 2003.

89   Communication from Manuel Herrera, January 24, 2002.

90   Communication from Kathleen Osowski, May 20, 2000.

91   Communication from Manuel Herrera, June 15, 2002.

92   Author interview with Manuel Herrera, May 1999.

93   Ibid.

94   Communication from Manuel Herrera, June 15, 2002.

95   Author interview with Manuel Herrera, May 1999.

96   Frank Cushing to Ed Linn, undated, Ed Linn papers.

97   Ibid.

98   Both Ballinger and Cushing are quotes in notes in the Ed Linn papers.

99   Communication from Manuel Herrera, September 3, 2001.

100   Barry Lorge, San Diego Union, July 7, 1991.

101   Undated Don Freeman column, San Diego Union.

102   Author interview with Joe Villarino, May 9, 1997.

103   Communication from Manuel Herrera, May 20, 2000. The notion of May Williams as a Mother Teresa figure comes from Manuel. In an October 1, 2000 note, he wrote, "May never got the credit for raising her family alone and much more in a country full of Depression! She did more with a Bible than Ted with baseball. If the country accepted women preaching the streets in the 1910's, 20's, 30's, 40's or even the 50's, then she would have been a Mother Teresa to America. May Williams was just too early for public praise or the advertising media of today! I feel very strongly about Aunt May and her quest to deliver the Word of God in the Depths of Sin. Believe me, there were many whom May Williams led to the promises of Jesus. Her goal: Salvation and your name written in the Book of Life. Ted was ashamed of his mother; I wish I had a mother who cared for me!"

104   Communications from Manuel Herrera, February 25, 2000 and September 3, 2001.

105   Conversation at Dee Allen's house, March 2003.

106   Communication from Manuel Herrera, November 4, 2002.

107   Communication from Manuel Herrera, February 16, 2000.

108   Interview with Manuel Herrera, May 1999.

109   Communication from Manuel Herrera, May 25, 1999.

110   Interview with Ted Williams, November 23, 2002.

111   Communication from Ted Williams, December 27, 2003.

112   Author interview with Sarah Diaz, May 1999.

113   Communication from Manuel Herrera, April 30, 2000. Manuel clearly had Ted in mind.

114   Author interview with Sarah Diaz, May 1999, and communication from Manuel Herrera, June 2, 1999.

115   Communication from Manuel Herrera, April 30, 2000.

116   Communication from Manuel Herrera, October 23, 2000.

117   Interview with Sarah Diaz, May 1999. Sarah's reference to the Japanese attack reminds us that there were two Japanese attacks on the continental United States during the Second World War. There was a February 28, 1942 shelling by a submarine near the Bankline Refinery oil field at Goleta and two airborne attempts to drop incendiary bombs in Oregon forests on September 9 and 10, 1942. Ron Kurtus says that the Goleta attack may have been a personal mission for the sub commander, who had been a ship captain who docked at Santa Barbara in the late 1930s and suffered a real loss of face. He was given a tour of the area, and "as the captain was admiring some scenery on a hillside, he backed up and lost his footing. He fell backwards into a bed of cactus! His guests burst into laughter at his misfortune. The captain did not understand the American sense of humor and felt that

he was being ridiculed by these people. He vowed to get revenge on Americans and on Santa Barbara." Returning as commander of a submarine, he shelled the pier and also the nearby oil field, but no one was injured and virtually no damage was done. However, the captain did gain a measure of revenge. Ron Kurtus, "When the Japanese Attacked Santa Barbara," found on the Internet at www.school-for-champions.com/history/sbattack.htm.

118 Communication from Manuel Herrera, May 29, 1999.

119 Author interview with Teresa Cordero Contreras, May 28, 2000.

120 Author interview with Teresa Cordero Contreras, December 29, 2003.

121 Author interview with Mary Redding, May 16, 2000.

122 Author interview with Teresa Cordero Contreras, May 28, 2000.

123 Ibidem.

124 Communication from Manuel Herrera, June 7, 2000.

125 Author interview with Teresa Cordero Contreras, December 29, 2003.

126 Communication from Manuel Herrera, June 7, 2000.

127 Communication from Manuel Herrera, December 27, 2000.

128 Author interview with Teresa Cordero Contreras, December 29, 2003.

129 Communication from Manuel Herrera, June 7, 2000.

130 Communication from Mary Redding, November 26, 2002.

131 Communication from Manuel Herrera, October 13, 2001.

132 Author interview with Danny Venzor, December 29, 2003.

133 Communications from Manuel Herrera, April 15, 2000 and May 2, 2000.

134 One can find his name listed among those California men killed in the war, in the Riverside Daily Press, December 24, 1918.

135 Author interview with Frank Venzor, May 15 & 18, 2000.

136 Communication from Manuel Herrera, October 11, 2000.

137 Ibid.

138 Communication from Manuel Herrera, June 7, 2002.

139 Author interview with Ruth Gonzales, February 28, 2003.

140 Communication from Manuel Herrera, June 9, 1999.

141 Communication from Manuel Herrera, May 31, 1999.

142 Communication from Manuel Herrera, June 9, 1999.

143 Saul C. Venzor obituary, *Santa Barbara News-Press*, August 16, 1963.

144 Author interview with Sarah Diaz, May 1999.

145 Author interview with Danny Venzor, December 28, 2003.

146 Communications from Manuel Herrera, May 7 and May 19, 2000.

147 Ibid.

148 Author interview with Frank Venzor, May 19, 2000.

149 Author interview with Rosalie Larson, March 2, 2003.

150 Communication from Manuel Herrera, April 3, 2000. Attempts to confirm that Saul Venzor faced Babe Ruth at any time have so far proven fruitless.

151 Interview with Frank Venzor, May 19, 2000.

152 John Zant, article in the *Santa Barbara News-Press*, July 6, 2002.

153 Ibid.

154 Author interview with Dee Allen, December 29, 2003.

155 John Zant, op. cit.

156 Communications from Manuel Herrera, May 4, 2000 and January 26, 2002. Danny Venzor scoffs at the story that Saul gave up a chance to play baseball for love. "Oh, that's bullshit! Not in my opinion. If a young guy like that has a chance, he's going to go. And coming from a poor Mexican family, to have a chance like that...there's going to be more than *that* to stop a guy from going." Author interview with Danny Venzor, December 28, 2003.

157 Author interview with Frank Venzor, May 15 & 18, 2000.

158 Communications from Manuel Herrera, June 9, 1999 and December 27, 2000.

159 Author interview with Dee Allen, December 29, 2003.

160 Communication from Manuel Herrera, May 19, 2000.

161   Communication from Manuel Herrera, June 16, 2002.

162   John Zant, *Santa Barbara News-Press*, op. cit. The stranger "poked his head in the door while we were having breakfast, saying he was looking for the elevator. He was looking to check out. He had gotten off on the wrong floor." Author interview with Danny Venzor, op. cit.

163   Communication from Manuel Herrera, June 16, 2002.

164   Communication from Manuel Herrera, May 16 & 17, 2002.

165   Interview with Charles Venzor, April 17, 2002. Chaz grew up with his mother, after his parents divorced, and never played baseball other than a bit at school. But Dee played some. She was a third baseman on a number of softball teams that she joined after she'd graduated school. She allowed as how she was a good runner, but she also had some of that hand-eye coordination. "I was the leadoff hitter because I could usually hit the ball." Dee played for a few years against teams from Oxnard and Ventura and other communities until about age 25 or so. "Did you ever imagine yourself as Ted Williams?" "Oh, no!" There was no such fantasy at play. Paul Venzor's daughter Rozie used to play some, too, and thinks she maybe played against Dee at one point. Like her famous uncle, Rozie played left field. "I really can't say I was that good," she laughed. "But it was fun." Ted's name was invoked, though. Rozie reports that once or twice Aunt Madeline used to yell out at her while she was up at the plate, "Do a Ted Williams!!" Conversation with Dee Allen and Rosalie Larson in Santa Barbara, March 2, 2003.

166   Author interview with Ted Williams on April 28, 2000.

167   Author interview with Sarah Diaz, May 1999.

168   Interview with Sam Williams, August 14, 2002.

169   Sarah makes it sound as though May received a commission on each copy of the magazine she sold. I am assured that Salvation Army soldiers do not.

170   Interview with Sarah Diaz, op. cit. Ruth Gonzalez says that when Ted first started playing with the San Diego Padres, May mailed newspaper writeups to the Ponce family in El Paso.

171   Forrest Warren, "I'd Ruther Be Ruth," Boston Globe, September 8, 1946. One hopes that May didn't click off her radio after the home run; Ted went 4-for-4 with two home runs.

172   Author interview with Sarah Diaz, op. cit.

173   Communication from Manuel Herrera, June 6, 1999.

174   Communication from Manuel Herrera, June 7, 2002.

175   Author interview with Teresa Cordero Contreras, December 29, 2003.

176   Author interview with Frank Venzor, May 15 & 18, 2000.

177   Communication from Rosalie Larson, December 13, 2003.

178   Ibid.

179   Communication from Manuel Herrera, May 19, 2000.

180   Communication from Manuel Herrera, June 7, 2002.

181   Author interview with Frank Venzor, May 15 & 18, 2000.

182   Communication from Manuel Herrera, July 26, 2002.

183   Communication from Manuel Herrera, May 31, 1999.

184   Communication with Ted Williams, March 2003.

185   Communication with Manuel Herrera, June 7, 2000.

186   Author interview with Danny Venzor May 7, 2000.

187   Author interview with Danny Venzor, May 7, 2000.

188   Interviews with Danny Venzor, May 7, 2000 and December 28, 2003. It wasn't that Bruno expected his son to become the next Ted Williams. "But he wanted me to play some ball. Professional. Just make the Coast League. A good living."

189   Communication from Manuel Herrera, June 3, 1999.

190   Communication from Manuel Herrera, May 19, 2000,

191   Author interview with Danny Venzor, op. cit. There is a stretch of roadway near San Diego named the Ted Williams Freeway.

192   Leigh Montville, *Ted Williams* (New York: Doubleday, 2004), 18.

193   Communication from Manuel Herrera, May 12, 2000.

194   Author interview with Dr. Howard Winet, November 23, 2002.

195   Ibid.

196   Ibid.

197   Communication from Mary Redding, November 26, 2002.

198   Communication from Manuel Herrera, October 12, 2001.

199   Communication from Manuel Herrera, May 2, 2000.

200   Communication from Howard Winet, December 5, 2003.

201   Ed Linn, Hitter, op. cit., 17, 18.

202   Ibid., pp. 32-33. Later, on page 72, Linn termed him a "rotten brother." Even with the assistance
of California corrections officials, it has been impossible to confirm that Danny Williams ever served time in San
Quentin.

203   Steve Corey, "Why Ted Williams Plays It Cool," *Uncensored*, August 1961.

204   Linn, Hitter, op. cit., 324-5.

205   Ted Williams, *My Turn At Bat*, 31-32.

206   Ibid., 32. Manuel Herrera believed that Danny had taken his own life with that pistol, but the fact that he'd
been in the hospital for seven days prior to this death would suggest otherwise. His son Sam states for a fact that
Danny died in the hospital.

207   Author interview with Sarah Diaz, May 1999.

208   Author interview with Manuel Herrera, May 29, 1999.

209   Author interview with Teresa Cordero Contreras interview, May 30, 2000.

210   Communication from Manuel Herrera, June 2, 2000.

211   Communication from Manuel Herrera, June 13, 2000.

212   Ibid.

213   Interview with Joe Villarino, May 9, 1997.

214   Steve Corey, "Why Ted Williams Plays It Cool," op. cit.

215   Author interview with Leonard Bell, September 19, 2003.

216   Author interview with Ted Williams, November 23, 2002.

217   Ibid.

218   Author interview with Jan Williams, February 2003.

219   Author interview with Ted Williams, November 23, 2002. One is reminded, of course, that Danny's father's
military record reflected "no unauthorized absence of record."

220   Communications from Manuel Herrera, May 3, 2000 and July 21, 2002.

221   Author interview with Sam Williams, August 14, 2002.

222   Author interview with Ted Williams, November 23, 2002.

223   Ibid. Sam added a note while editing this piece for first publication, in May 2004: "Yeah - that was really
fun."

224   Ibid.

225   Ibid.

226   Author interview with Sam Williams, August 14, 2002.

227   Author interview with Ted Williams, November 23, 2002.

228   Ibid.

229   Ibid.

230   Ibid.

231   Communication from Manuel Herrera, May 3, 2000. If the pistol was for protection against union
partisans, he may have overcome the need. He and Jean lived for some time at 716 West Grace Street in Chicago,
and Danny was initiated into the Brotherhood of Painters, Decorators and Paperhangers I.U. 147 on September
9, 1957, per a union book in his son's possession. "He liked guns and books about guns," Ted recalls. "I remember
him strapping his pistol on the steering column of the car whenever we traveled some distance, and him getting
busted for it once." Communication from Ted Williams, August 24, 2002.

232   Communication from Manuel Herrera, July 2, 2000.

233   Author interview with Manuel Herrera, May 29, 1999 and communication dated July 2, 2000.

234   Communication from Manuel Herrera, July 2, 2000 and interview May 29, 1999.

235   Communication from Manuel Herrera, July 3, 2000.

236   Communication from Ted Williams, September 8, 2003.

237   Communication from Ted Williams, August 24, 2002.

238   Ibid.

239   Steve Connolly, "Time with son made Kid happy," *Boston Herald*, July 14, 2002.

240   Claudia Williams, *Ted Williams, My Father* (New York: Ecco Press, 2014), 9.

241   Author interview with Steve Brown, July 19, 2004.

242   Communications from Manuel Herrera, May 31, 1999 and January 12, 2004.

243   Communication from Manuel Herrera, May 2, 2000.

244   Interview with Gene Bowman, January 19, 2004.

245   Author interview with Gabriel Arellanes, January 19, 2004.

246   Author interview with Greg Venzor, February 19, 2004.

247   Author interviews with Davey Gonzalez and Ruth Gonzalez, February 19, 2004.

248   Ibid.

249   Author interview with Peter Gammons, December 1, 2014.

250   Anthony J. Connor, *Baseball for the Love Of It* (New York: Macmillan, 1982), quoted in *Prime & Nowlin, Ted Williams: The Pursuit of Perfection* (Chicago: Sports Publishing, 200), 239. See also *Washington Post*, July 10, 1971.

251   Ben Bradlee Jr. interview with Al Cassidy, December 5, 2002. Ben Bradlee, Jr., *The Kid: The Immortal Life of Ted Williams*, op. cit., 26.

252   Author interview with Mary Redding, May 2000.

253   Author interview with Howard Winet, November 23, 2002. As we have seen, Dr. Winet's family had changed their name from Winetski, because of another form of prejudice.

254   Author interview with Connie Matthews, November 26 & December 10, 2002.

255   Author interview with Ruth Gonzales, February 28, 2003.

256   Frank Venzor, in conversation at Dee Allen's house in Santa Barbara, March 2003. Manuel Herrera told essentially the same story in communications on May 3 and June 2, 2000. Madeline's sister Teresa confirmed the story and Ted's words. Asked if she thought Ted's outburst reflected some embarrassment to be associated with Hispanic or Indian people, she said, "I don't think so. He was so upset with her. I don't think he was prejudiced. He never appeared to me like he was. He loved my dad, and my dad, well, he was Indian. He was Indian and Spanish. Ted would come over and they'd talk. My mom would shoo us out. 'Little kids, get out of here' and they would speak. I can't see him being unrespectful or anything." Author interview with Teresa Cordero Contreras, December 29, 2003. I also spoke to Ruth Gonzales on February 19, 2004 and she said, about Ted, "He didn't claim any relatives" (meaning that he kept his relatives at arm's length.) I asked about Sarah Diaz, and she said Sarah was the exception. "She was the only one that Ted wanted to see. Ted would tell Sarah, 'Don't tell anybody. If you do, I will never come and visit you again.' Some of her cousins, when May died, wanted to go see Ted Williams. He had a private funeral. They didn't say anything much about May; they just wanted to see Ted Williams."

257   Author interview with David Ronquillo, October 23, 2003. There is no evidence that the Red Sox did offer such advice to young Williams.

258   Ibid. Manuel Herrera adds that when they cleaned out the Utah Street one time, Ted destroyed all the pictures at home. "Ted was ashamed and tore up the damn pictures, then he laughed it off." Communication from Manuel Herrera, April 30, 2000.

259   Interview with David Ronquillo, November 24, 2003. David found some papers his own mother had written, telling about experiences of discrimination she had experienced. "When my mother first went into the missionary field, she was severely discriminated against. As a result, she convinced my dad – who was very Hispanic and very proud of his Hispanic heritage – to move into a kind of Anglo environment. My mother, I think, was very conscious of all this. I'm just speculating that May may have been in the same situation. When I began school, I couldn't speak English. My grandmother lived with us, who would have been May Williams' aunt, I believe. My dad was more comfortable speaking Spanish, more comfortable than speaking English. My mother was fully bilingual. But I realize by reading my mother's memoirs that she really went through a period of time when she was severely discriminated against and I think she really wanted to see her children integrated into the Anglo environment so that they didn't have to go through that." David adds his observation that there are "far more people in our family from my generation that don't speak any Spanish than there are those that speak Spanish. From what I'm gathering, May spoke English very well, and my guess was that that was the only language spoken at home for Ted."

260   Author interview with Ruth Gonzales, February 28, 2003. Ruth herself was a bilingual instructional aide at

Los Cerritos Grammar School in the City of Paramount for 20 years, so she was attuned to questions of the use of language.

261   Interview with Maureen Surratt, January 5, 2004. Maureen and her husband farm near El Paso today, working a field just a block away from the Rio Grande. Ernest Ponce was the first Hispanic elected to the El Paso City Council, where he served from 1951 to 1957. He died March 15, 2002.

262   Author interview with Ted Williams, November 23, 2002.

263   Ibid.

264   Author interview with Teresa Cordero Contreras, May 28, 2000.

265   Interview with David Ronquillo, November 24, 2003. Times have changed. David is proud of his heritage, and Ted's nephew Ted wrote me, "According to Danny, Ted liked to call the rest of the family 'the Mexicans,' though I think it was more jokingly than serious. May always said they were Spanish, not Mexican, of course. I always liked the idea of being part Mexican: seemed very romantic!" Communication from Ted Williams, October 29, 2002.

266   Author interview with Ruth Gonzales, February 28, 2003.

267   Author interview with Joe Villarino, May 9 & July 5, 1997.

268   Communication from Leigh Montville, February 26, 2004.

269   Author interview with Frank Cushing, January 24, 2004.

270   Author interview with Larry Doby, January 14, 1997.

271   Ted Williams, syndicated column written December 13, 1962.

272   Tito Avila, email to author, January 15, 2018.

273   New York Times, August 26, 2005.

274   J.A. Marzán, "Ted Williams: Throw the Heat; Hold the Tortillas," *New English Review,* November 2014.

275   Adrian Burgos, Jr., "No, Ted Williams Was Not Baseball's First Latino Superstar," *The Sporting News,* June 24, 2015.

276   Jesse Sanchez, "Clemente Heads All-Time Latino Team," MLB.com, September 25, 2012. http://mlb.mlb.com/mlb/events/alltimelatino/index.jsp

www.ingramcontent.com/pod-product-compliance
Lightning Source LLC
LaVergne TN
LVHW051514080426
835509LV00017B/2057